ROCK & ROLL
and the
ROCK OF AGES

PAYING HOMAGE TO THE ULTIMATE REBEL

FRANK GARROTT

Rock & Roll and the Rock of Ages
Paying Homage to the Ultimate Rebel
Frank Garrott

To contact the author:
info@frankgarrott.com

Edited by:

Mary Ethel

Mary Ethel Eckard
Frisco, Texas

Library of Congress Control Number: 2025902353
ISBN (Paperback): 978-1-966561-04-0
ISBN (Hardcover): 978-1-966561-07-1
ISBN (E-book): 978-1-966561-05-7

DEDICATION

This book is dedicated to my mom, who has exemplified gratitude and perseverance; to my dad, who modeled what a father should be; to my children and their spouses, who have a zest for life; and especially to my wife, who is the centerpiece of our family zaniness.

ACKNOWLEDGEMENTS

When someone undertakes a project that seems a little crazy, those closest to that person can react in one of two ways. Often, the circle of family and friends will be polite and offer a metaphorical pat on the head while doubting the sanity of the one embarking on the project. On the other hand, many who surround him or her may be very genuine encouragers even if they have their reservations.

In writing this book, I have been encouraged by several people who may have scratched their heads a bit at a book by a first-time author intersecting the life of Jesus and rock & roll music.

Here I express gratitude to my encouragers who have traveled the journey with me – Mike Wallis, Matt Maberry; my editor, Mary Ethel Eckard; my pastor, Charlie Dunn; colleagues Mike Douris and Kelli Schwartz. Last but certainly not least, I thank my wife Lynne who was a consistent encourager when she could have just rolled her eyes. (Maybe she did when I wasn't looking!)

I'm reminded of another project a few thousand years ago where family and friends probably thought the builder was a bit loony – Noah's ark. Noah persevered and the family did get in the ark. My short book pales in comparison to building a huge ark. The relevance to me today is to appreciate encouragers and avoid mockers. I am grateful that I had many of the former and none of the latter.

CONTENTS

SECTION III

INTRODUCTION

WHAT'S THE BEST concert you've ever attended? Reflecting on your answer to this question can bring back fond memories and sometimes spark a lighthearted debate in social outings. Let's keep going with the questions:

- What rock & roll song most defined the era? (1964-1977. I get to define the years; it's my book.)
- What was the best rock & roll song?
- What was the best rock & roll album?
- What was the best rock & roll song that included a reference to Jesus?

Wait a second. What was that last bullet point? Yes, I said Jesus, the Rock of Ages. In this period of rebellion as reflected in protest marches, the drug culture and provocative lyrics in many songs, the number of bands and artists that made references to Jesus and aspects of the Christian faith may surprise you.

As I read and contemplated the lyrics through the biblical lens which informs my world view, I concluded that most of the artists got it somewhat right and a few nailed it. Admittedly, I don't know the hearts of those who penned the words. There is no judgment; I'm simply basing my views on the lyrics supplemented by basic internet research to capture background of the artists, bands, and songs. Their lyrics take us on a rollercoaster journey of spiritual twists and turns.

This book devotes a chapter to each of nine well-known songs across the spectrum of rock & roll and offers a critique that is at once serious and lighthearted.

So, who am I writing this book for? Anyone who wants to read it! Who I had in mind when the thoughts first started to percolate was the long-haired, tie-dyed Boomer with an interest in spiritual matters, but a skepticism about Jesus. From there, my hope was, and is, that the appeal of what I have written would overcome the generational chasm because of the familiarity of the songs chosen.

By the way, my answers to the first three questions posed in the opening paragraph can be found in Appendix I.

Section I

We begin our journey
eager for spiritual clarity.
These songwriters
start on the right path,
but occasionally
get sidetracked.

CHAPTER 1

"Spirit in the Sky"

by Norman Greenbaum

AFTER THE FIRST few notes, many Baby Boomers can identify "Spirit in the Sky." Even though it was released over 50 years ago (1969), its appeal is cross-generational. That's in part because the song has appeared in over 30 commercials and more than 60 movies. Funeral directors have commented that it is one of the most requested songs at funeral services because it offers encouragement to family and friends that the deceased is going to "go to the place that's best."

His Life

Because the lyrics refer to Jesus, one might assume that Greenbaum is an evangelical Christian. He's not;

he was raised in an orthodox Jewish family in Malden, Massachusetts and remains an observant Jew to this day.

Although there were other influences that stirred his mind to imagine the contours of this song, the trigger was when he watched Porter Wagoner on television performing a gospel song. That motivated Greenbaum to see if he could write his own gospel song. In interviews, he explains that the words came easily; he wrote "Spirit in the Sky" in 15 minutes. It became a worldwide hit, topping the charts throughout Europe, Australia and Canada, and reached #3 in the U.S. in April 1970.

Greenbaum moved to Los Angeles in 1965 to embark on a music career. He has been referred to as a one-hit wonder, which may not be entirely fair as a couple of other songs he wrote just missed the Top 40 lists.

Nonetheless, he left the music business in 1972 and returned to his dairy farm. He went back to the music industry in the mid-80's as a manager and promoter.

Greenbaum still performs. He celebrated his 80th birthday in 2022 with a performance at the Ryman Auditorium in Nashville.

"Spirit in the Sky" – The Song [1]

Now on to the song that made him famous. Here are the lyrics relevant for our purposes:

When I die and they lay me to rest
Gonna go to the place that's best

When I lay me down to die
Goin' up to the spirit in the sky

Prepare yourself; you know it's a must
Gotta have a friend in Jesus
So you know that when you die
He's gonna recommend you to the spirit in the sky

Never been a sinner; I never sinned
I got a friend in Jesus [2]

What Does the Bible Say

Greenbaum got off to a great start. When we die, that's not the end of the story. That's good news. The other side of that coin is that we are accountable for our life on earth – what we believed and how our actions reflected that belief. God is a Righteous Judge and will judge us based on our faith in His Son, Jesus.

Greenbaum recognizes that he wants to "go up to the spirit in the sky." The Bible calls that Heaven, but I'm not going to quibble with his term. (I don't particularly care for the expression "the man upstairs," but I recognize that's a casual reference to God.) In similar fashion, Greenbaum recognizes he wants to spend eternity in a good place; the best place!

Then he really hits his stride when he encourages listeners to prepare themselves. This is certainly consistent with biblical exhortation. Luke 12:35 tells the reader: "Be dressed in readiness and keep your lamps alight." Later in the book of Luke, we read: "Be on guard that our hearts may not be weighted down" (21:34). And "keep on the alert at all times" (21:36). Matthew 25:13 echoes the same sentiment: "Be on the alert." In fact, the theme of preparedness runs through the Gospels and the entire New Testament.

The words of the song speak to the listener, telling him or her how to prepare themselves – by having a friend in Jesus. The beauty of this lyric is the recognition of the possibility of a personal relationship with God's Son. Jesus certainly wants to be your friend. In John 15:15, Jesus tells His disciples "I have called you friends." That same opportunity is ours today. Two verses back, He tells them (and us): "Greater love has no one than this, that one lay down his life for his friends." That's what Jesus did.

If we respond to Jesus's offer to be our friend, as well as Lord and Savior, then He's "gonna recommend us to the spirit in the sky." Once again, Greenbaum nailed it. Matthew 10:32 reads: "Every one therefore who shall confess Me before men, I will also confess him before My Father who is in Heaven." Sounds like "recommending" to me.

However, biblically speaking, Greenbaum does stumble once – in the last stanza: "Never been a sinner; I've never sinned." We all know intuitively that we have sinned, and we are sinners. Romans 3:23 says: "For all have sinned and fall short of the glory of God." Psalm 14:1 reinforces this notion: "The fool has said in his heart 'There is no God. There is no one who does good.'"

If we weren't sinners, we could get to the "spirit in the sky" on the basis of our good life – making sure our credits outnumber our debits. But that's not how it works. We "gotta have a friend in Jesus" so we can be confident that He's "gonna recommend us to the spirit in the sky," His Father.

In interviews with Greenbaum, I read that some Christians were upset with his line about sinners. Hey, it's his song. I choose to focus on the lyrics where the listener is encouraged to be prepared for death, to have a friend in Jesus, and to be confident that He will be your advocate when it really matters – on Judgment Day.

A Final Word

Norman, if you read this, thank you for your song. Even though it probably wasn't your intent, I bet there are many folks in Heaven because they contemplated your lyrics and responded to the message, which is the invitation Jesus offers in Matthew 11:28: "Come to Me, all who are weary and heavy-laden, and I will give you rest."

Norman, I pray that when your time on earth is up, that you "go to the place that's best." Perhaps there will be a corner lot with a good view in Heaven for a Jew who wrote a song about having a friend in Jesus.

CHAPTER 2

"Sympathy for the Devil"

by Mick Jagger and The Rolling Stones

1968: A YEAR of turmoil in the U.S. and around the world – riots, political turbulence and mass civil unrest. The assassinations of Martin Luther King, Jr. and Robert Kennedy, violence at the Democratic National Convention in Chicago, the Soviet Union invasion of Prague to crack down on reformists. These are just a few of the tumultuous events of that year.

It's only fitting that on December 6, The Rolling Stones released a new album, "Beggars Banquet" with the opening song "Sympathy for the Devil. [3]

The Rolling Stones – A Little Background

For over 60 years, much has been written about Mick Jagger and The Rolling Stones, so here as background we'll simply offer a few facts and anecdotes.

- The Rolling Stones got their start in London in 1962.
- The band is the 4th best-selling group of all time.
- They performed over 2,000 concerts around the world.
- They produced 30 studio albums; 23 live albums, and over 340 songs.

The originals, Jagger and guitarist Keith Richards, were childhood friends. Jagger moved away and they reconnected in 1961. Charlie Watts, the band's drummer who died in 2021, joined Jagger and Richards in 1963, a few months after they performed their first show.

Brian Jones has been referred to as "the uncontested leader of the band" in the early years. In fact, he named the band during a phone call with The Jazz News. When asked by a journalist for the band's name, Jones saw a Muddy Waters LP lying on the floor; one of the tracks was "Rollin' Stones." That was a stroke of luck! Jones succumbed to drugs and died in 1969. Bass guitarist Ronnie Wood joined the Stones in 1975 and still performs with them to this day. Several others drifted in and out, but these are the mainstays.

Mick Jagger - More Than the Image

Jagger grew up in Dartford, Kent in the UK. His bad-boy persona is based on facts – 8 children with 5 women, drug usage, jail time, etc. But that's not the whole story. He studied at the London School of Economics where he took finance and accounting courses. He has called his father, who was a gymnast and a physical education teacher, the greatest influence in his life. He was likely amazed to see his son knighted in 2002 – Sir Michael Philip Jagger.

He and the band were staunch supporters of the civil rights movement in America. He negotiated a clause in their contracts where they would refuse to perform in segregated venues.

While Jagger and Richards have had a rollercoaster relationship, they still perform together. This would have surprised Jagger in 1975 when he was quoted as saying: "I'd rather be dead than singing 'Satisfaction' when I'm 45." Glad he's still alive and still singing "Satisfaction" in sold-out stadiums around the world.

Origins of "Sympathy for the Devil"

In 1968, a few months removed from an arrest for drug possession, Jagger was reading poetry and philosophy.

The initial seed for the song was planted as he read a French poet from the 1800's named Charles Baudelaire.

One of his famous quotes was: "The devil's finest trick is to persuade you that he does not exist."

The seed planted in Jagger's mind was nourished by reading a novel his girlfriend gave him, Mikhail Bulgakov's "The Master and Margarita." Bulgakov took 12 years to write the book, finished in 1940. The Russian government banned it, but it was finally released in 1967. The storyline is the devil and his minions roaming around Moscow in the 1930's, creating mayhem. It ridiculed Soviet leaders and the government bureaucracy. More specifically, it was written as a critique of atheistic propaganda and the denial of God in the USSR. There are references in the book to Jesus and Pontius Pilate. No wonder it was banned!

Perhaps not surprisingly, rumors spread that Jagger and the Stones were devil worshippers. In fact, they were exposers of the devil, as reflected by this Keith Richards quote years later: "You might as well accept the fact that evil is there and deal with it any way you can. 'Sympathy for the Devil' is a song that says: 'Don't forget him. If you confront him, then he's out of a job.'"

"Sympathy for the Devil" – The Song

Before we look at the lyrics, let's consider the title. On the one hand, there is the acknowledgement that the devil is real by whatever name he is called – Satan, Lucifer, the Deceiver, the Father of Lies. In fact, Richards' quote above reinforces this notion, suggesting that it is wise to acknowledge his existence and naïve to do otherwise. According to a 2023 Gallup poll, 58% of Americans do accept the reality of the devil.

At a deeper level, this reflects the reality of spiritual warfare which has existed since Adam and Eve were wandering around the Garden of Eden. As the personification of evil and deception, Satan has ruined the lives of millions upon millions of people through the centuries and deserves disdain, contempt, disgust, loathing; anything but our sympathy.

While the lyrics are familiar to many, they are reproduced here in truncated form, leaving out repetitive stanzas and minimizing references to historical events that are not relevant to the point of this chapter.

Please allow me to introduce myself
I'm a man of wealth and taste
I've been around for long, long years
Stole many a man's soul and faith

And I was 'round when Jesus Christ
Had his moment of doubt and pain
Made damn sure that Pilate
Washed his hands and sealed his fate

Pleased to meet you
Hope you guessed my name
But what's puzzlin' you
Is the nature of my game [4]

The devil introduces himself as one who is cultured and sophisticated, and at the same time acknowledges that he stole many a man's soul and faith.

What Does the Bible Say?

In John 10:10, Jesus says "I came that they might have life and might have it abundantly." Less often quoted is the first part of the same verse, which reads: "The thief comes only to steal, kill and destroy." In this regard, the opening stanza of "Sympathy" is consistent with scripture. The devil exists to suck the life, the soul out of men and women. In Matthew 16:26, Jesus challenges His disciples: "For what will a man be profited if he gains the whole world but forfeits his soul?" Soul – the very essence of life, which the devil seeks to steal, kill and destroy.

In the second stanza, the devil brags that he was there when Jesus had his moment of doubt and pain, and he made sure that Pilate washed his hands and sealed His fate.

The writer of this song must have known, or at least consulted, his Bible. Jesus did have His moment of doubt and pain in the Garden of Gethsemane (Mark 14:34-36). Given our awareness of spiritual warfare, it is reasonable to conclude that the devil was there at this pivotal moment in human history.

After Gethsemane and Judas's betrayal, Jesus was brought before Pilate who did what he could to avoid sentencing Jesus to death. But under great pressure from all sides, he gave in to the crowd, but not before he washed his hands and declared "I am innocent of this man's blood" (Matthew 27:24). He knew who Jesus was. John 19:19 tells us: "Pilate wrote an inscription and put it on the cross. It was written 'Jesus the Nazarene, the King of the Jews.' The chief priest asked him to amend it to 'He said I am the King of the Jews.' Pilate responded (verse 22) 'What I have written I have written.'"

Although Pilate seems to have recognized that Jesus was no ordinary man, when he washed his hands, he did in fact seal his own fate. And yet, he merely sealed Jesus's physical fate – death by crucifixion. But as the centerpiece of God's grand plan of redemption of His creation, Jesus defeated death, was resurrected and assumed His place at the right hand of God. The only fate that is sealed, besides Pilate's, is that of those who choose to ignore or reject Jesus, those who do not grapple with the question He asked His disciples: "But who do you say that I am?" (Matthew 16:15)

Underlying this discussion and the whole arena of spiritual warfare is a simple question: Do you believe in the unseen world? II Corinthians 4:18 says "We look not at the things which are seen, but at the things which are not seen; for the things which are seen are temporal, but the things which are not seen are eternal." I believe that each one of us has a sense of the eternal, of the unseen in our hearts. The writer of Ecclesiastes (3:11) puts it this way: God who created us "set eternity in our hearts."

Providing an answer to the question about your belief in the unseen world is an excellent starting point on the journey of faith. An affirmative response makes plausible a creator God who intervenes in the lives of His creation, the ultimate intervention sending His Son to earth, where in fact Pilate did not seal His fate.

The Devil's Schemes

In the third stanza, the devil says: "What's puzzlin' you is the nature of my game." Once again, the songwriter demonstrates consistency with Scripture. The devil is slick and crafty; we can be fooled by his lies and deception. However, the Bible does provide us clues as to his wicked ways. Refer back to John 10:10 – "The thief comes only to steal, kill and destroy." Do you sometimes feel the life being drained from you? Perhaps it is the devil. He is called the Deceiver and the Father of Lies. Our intuition often reveals to us when we are being duped, deceived, and lied to. Be attuned to the possibility that there is an unseen battle for your soul – one side seeking to give you the abundant life and the other side working to rob you of peace and joy. We really shouldn't be "puzzled by the nature of his game," especially if we read and internalize God's word, seek His guidance and surround ourselves with wise, discerning friends.

In "The Screwtape Letters," C.S. Lewis uses satire to introduce us to Screwtape and Wormwood. Screwtape, high up in the devil's hierarchy, advises his nephew, Wormwood, a novice demon, on how to keep the young man to whom he has been assigned from becoming a Christian. Wormwood fails, so Uncle Screwtape turns his attention to coaching Wormwood on ways to ensure the young man becomes distracted and disillusioned about his faith. The humor alone is worth the read, but more importantly, Lewis's classic offers real insight as to how the devil and his minions operate to separate us from our creator and make our lives miserable.

In the preface to the book, Lewis offers this counsel: "There are two equal and opposite errors into which our race can fall about the devils. One is to disbelieve in their existence. The other is to believe, and to feel an excessive and unhealthy interest in them. [5]

The Rest of the Song

As noted earlier, the lyrics of "Sympathy" make several references to historical events outside the scope and intent of this chapter, including the 1917 Bolshevik revolution, Hitler's decimation of Poland, the assassinations of the Kennedys and other devastation. The words of the entire song are so powerful and leave the unmistakable impression that the devil had a hand in evil plans executed by evil men who upended the world. Were Hitler, Stalin and others taken over by the devil? Or did the devil merely whisper in their ears and stir up the extreme wickedness that was already in their hearts? Or perhaps the devil sat back and just applauded their evil actions? Only God knows with perfect clarity what role the devil played and continues to play today. Spiritual warfare is a mystery, and it would be presumptive to suggest that the mystery will be unraveled this side of the grave. The purpose of this chapter is to demonstrate that spiritual warfare, the unseen world, and the devil, are real. Jagger's lyrics from start to finish do it brilliantly.

So, thank you Sir Mick for this fast-moving, thought-provoking contribution to the annals of rock & roll history. Even without the words, the music is worth a listen. But the words are profound. I don't know what you believe, but "Sympathy for the Devil" drives home the reality of spiritual warfare in an artful and compelling manner. I hope and pray the readers take note of the words you have written and are motivated to investigate what Scripture has to say about the devil, his efforts to come between us and our creator, and his ultimate doom.

CHAPTER 3

"Oh Lord, Won't You Buy Me a Mercedes Benz"

by Janis Joplin

CIVIL UNREST, CAMPUS protests, escalation of the drug culture did not end when the Times Square ball dropped on January 1, 1970. The first year of the new decade was marked by a war in Vietnam which appeared to have no end in sight, the Kent State massacre, and continued increase in violent crime. This was the environment for the last year of Janis Joplin's life.

Her Life and Death

Twenty-seven (27) – the number of years of a life cut short. Born in 1943 in Port Arthur, Texas; died in 1970 in

Hollywood, California. She lost a lengthy battle with heroin addiction, influenced by those who fueled her addiction and others who tried to free her from its stranglehold. Her death came just 16 days after Jimi Hendrix died of an overdose. Joplin died alone in the Landmark Motor Hotel in Hollywood. The date was October 4, 1970. Mark that date – we'll come back to it later.

In high school in Port Arthur, where she was a classmate of Hall of Fame football coach Jimmy Johnson, Joplin was ostracized and bullied. She called herself a "misfit." She attended Lamar University and the University of Texas, but did not graduate and appeared to suffer from the same ostracism. After she dropped out, Joplin headed to San Francisco, specifically the Haight-Ashbury neighborhood, a center of the drug culture of that era. Joplin had well-publicized relationships with men and women, several of whom betrayed her loyalty.

In the midst of a chaotic and what seems like a tragic life, she managed to write songs that have enjoyed remarkable staying power and to give electric performances in front of massive audiences. To get an idea of how her fame had spread by the age of 25, in 1968 she was the headline act at the Fillmore West in San Francisco; the opening acts were Chicago and Santana.

Joplin also performed at the Monterey Pop Festival, as well as Woodstock. She was inducted into the Rock & Roll Hall of Fame in 1995 and received a Grammy Lifetime Achievement Award in 2005.

Background of "Mercedes Benz"

(For all you grammar nerds like me, the company uses a dash; the song does not, so please don't email me about a typo.)

Joplin wrote the words at Vahsen's, a bar in Port Chester, New York, where she first sang it on August 8, 1970. Inspired by the first line of a song written by San Francisco poet Michael McClure, "Come on God and buy me a Mercedes-Benz," she composed it with Bob Neuwirth who wrote her words on a napkin at the bar and made a few of his own suggestions.

There are over 40 cover versions of the song. Mercedes-Benz has used the song in advertisements, most memorably during the 2011 Super Bowl.

Joplin completed her last recording of "Mercedes Benz" on October 1, 1970, just three days before she died.

"Mercedes Benz" – The Song [6]

Sometimes simpler is better. It's not a stretch to imagine the words of this song coming together in a bar in New York, where they were captured on a napkin. Lucky for us the bartender didn't take the napkin, wipe up the bar with it and toss it away. The focus for our purposes will be on the first two stanzas:

Oh Lord, won't you buy me
A Mercedes Benz?
My friends all drive Porsches
I must make amends

I worked hard all my lifetime
No help from my friends
Oh Lord, won't you buy me
A Mercedes Benz? [7]

Once Joplin got the Lord's attention with her request for an expensive car, she didn't stop there – petitioning Him next for a color TV and finally asking for "a night on the town," naturally with Him "buying the next round."

What Does the Bible Say?

"Oh Lord" – that's a good start! The Lord is pleased when His creation acknowledges Him and talks to Him. He encourages us to ask. Matthew 7:7 says: "Ask and it shall be given to you." So why not ask for a Mercedes-Benz or a color TV?

Two verses later, Jesus reinforces the promise by referring to a good father who, when his son asks for bread, would not instead give him a stone. Naturally, a loving father wants to be receptive to requests from his children.

There Is a Caveat

However, the Gospel of John, chapter 14; verse 14, throws a little cold water on the notion of God as an ATM machine by adding the phrase "in My name." Jesus tells His disciples: "If you ask Me anything in My name, I will do it."

"In My name" means consistent with My will. Prayers clearly inconsistent with the Lord's will won't be answered. As an example, if a wealthy man prays for a bigger yacht, that prayer will surely fall on deaf ears.

So, consider the request for a Mercedes-Benz. Maybe Joplin's car had been totaled and she was struggling financially, so if she was going to ask for a car, why not ask for the best? On the other hand, "a night on the town" as she likely meant it (booze- and drug-infused) is probably contrary to the Lord's will and not be "in His name."

The True God Hears

Joplin did petition the God who could actually answer her prayers. This is in contrast to any other supposed god. The distinction between a god who can answer prayer and a god who is silent (i.e., doesn't exist) is captured humorously in the story of Elijah and the prophets of Baal. They engage in a contest to see whose god will respond to a call for fire to come down from above.

I Kings 18 recounts the episode. Elijah, knowing he serves the living God, lets the prophets of Baal go first. Verse

26 tells us that there was no answer, so in the next verse, Elijah makes fun of them: "Call out with a loud voice, for he is a god; either he is occupied or gone aside or is on a journey or perhaps he is asleep and needs to be awakened." When it's Elijah's turn, he says "Answer me, O Lord, that this people may know that you, O Lord, are God." God answered; it didn't end well for the prophets of Baal.

Keep It Simple

Not only did Joplin petition the true God who could answer her prayer, but she did so in a simplistic, conversational manner that would likely have pleased the Lord. Contrast her words with the prayer of the Pharisee in Luke 18:11, "God, I thank thee that I am not like other people." No wonder Jesus called the Pharisees "white-washed tombs." Jesus and Elijah could talk trash.

Don't Negotiate with God

The simple prayer requests in Joplin's song do miss the mark in a couple of ways. She makes a reference to "working hard all my life with no help from my friends," the implication being that God should answer her material requests because of her works.

Christianity and, more specifically, salvation are not a matter of debits and credits. Thank God for that. We all fall short. (See Psalm 53, Romans 3:23.) And although many Christians, myself included, often treat prayer as a quid pro quo, that's not the way it works. Our simple minds think "I'll do this good act; then God, you respond accordingly." Fortunately, God's way is different. He prefers to lavish grace and mercy upon us in spite of the fact that we don't deserve it. Ephesians 2:8-9 reads: "For by grace you have been saved through faith, and that not of yourselves, it is the gift of God; not as a result of works, that no one should boast."

I'm not convinced that what she asked for was appropriate. In any event, I would have encouraged her to remake her appeal not on the basis of anything she had done, but rather on the basis of God's grace, fatherly love and generosity.

The Folly of the Prosperity Gospel

The other way in which the prayer requests miss the mark is the emphasis on expensive material goods.

The Lord does want to lavish gifts on those who believe in Him – spiritual gifts to use for the care and edification of our fellow man, fruits of the Spirit listed in Galatians 5:22-23 (love, joy, peace, patience, kindness, goodness, faithfulness, gentleness, self-control), and the abundant life that Jesus promises in John 10:10.

Sadly, the reference to an abundant life has often been misunderstood, sometimes influenced by deceitful pastors who have misled their congregations. Jesus never promises material gain; in fact, He promises the opposite. Christians are called to deny themselves (Matthew 16:24). I Peter 4:13, Romans 8:17, and Philippians 3:10 call believers to share in Jesus's sufferings. However, the Bible does promise contentment to those who believe. As Paul states in Philippians 4:11-12, "For I have learned to be content in whatever circumstances I am. I know how to get along with humble means, and I also know how to live in prosperity."

The purveyors of the "Prosperity Gospel" focus only on the latter part of this verse and misapply the word "abundant." Joplin may have been duped by the "Prosperity Gospel." I suspect she did not get her Mercedes-Benz.

This brings to mind the first part of the prayer of Jabez, where in I Chronicles 4:10, he asks God to bless him and enlarge his territory. In his book "The Prayer of Jabez," Bruce Wilkinson reminds us that Jabez wanted more influence, more responsibility and more opportunity to make a mark for God. He notes that Jabez left it entirely up to God to decide what the blessings would be and when, where and how he would receive them.

Wilkinson goes on to say, "This kind of radical trust in God's good intentions toward us has nothing in common with the popular gospel that you should ask God for a Cadillac *(or a Mercedes-Benz)* or some other material sign *(a color TV?)* that you have found a way to cash in on your connection with Him."[8]

A Final Word

I hope in the three days between the last recording of Mercedes Benz and Joplin's death that she may somehow have grasped the true meaning of the abundant life and petitioned the Lord to be her savior and rescuer. It's possible. Recall one of the greatest split-second decisions in the history of mankind – the criminal hanging on a cross next to Jesus with his request (Luke 23:42) – "Jesus, remember me when You come in Your kingdom." Jesus promised that on that very day, he would be with Him in Paradise.

A READER'S REST

THANKS FOR READING the first 3 chapters. I hope it's been worthwhile and peaks your interest to continue the journey. Like a traveler's rest, when I am reading a book, even a short one like this, I like to catch my breath after a few chapters and digest what I've read.

So before we move on to John Lennon's "Imagine," let's pause and take stock of what we have picked up from these opening chapters.

The artists spotlighted so far were obviously creative, perhaps brilliant, individuals on several levels. However, they made no claim to be theologians or biblical scholars.

And yet, they appear to have had an awareness of, or at least an intuition about, Jesus. Perhaps the connection was rebellion. Jesus was considered a rebel when He walked the earth 2000 years ago. He criticized, and even mocked, the establishment – the leaders of the Pharisees along with their burdensome rules.

The rebellion of the artists we have profiled so far has been well-chronicled. So, maybe it's not that surprising that each one would write a song about Jesus. There is a connection; there is something about Him that seems to have resonated.

Here are key takeaways from the creative lyrics, whether or not they intended to lead the listener to these conclusions:

"Spirit in the Sky" – Heaven

- Death is not the end; it does not have the final word.
- If there is life after death, we need to be prepared for it.
- Preparation for "going to the place that's best" is accepting Jesus was who He said He was; accepting His offer of friendship; and living a life that would prompt our friend to say, "Well done."
- If we do that, He will "recommend" us (be our advocate) to God, His Father.

"Sympathy for the Devil" – Spiritual Warfare

- Acknowledge that the devil is real.
- There is a constant battle for our souls.
- Belief in the unseen world in general is a logical starting point for belief more specifically in God, Heaven, Hell, angels and demons.
- Everyone needs to answer the most important question that Jesus posed: "But who do you say that I am?" Ignoring the question is also an answer, albeit an unfortunate one.

- The devil's tactics *are* puzzling but become clearer as we internalize God's word.

"Oh Lord, Won't You Buy Me a Mercedes Benz" – Prayer

- Ask boldly.
- If the request is contrary to God's will and to God's character, don't expect an answer.
- Ask the true God who can actually answer prayers.
- Avoid repetitious, pious prayers.
- Make your appeal to God on the basis of His character rather than your works.
- Lean your prayers toward spiritual blessings and other-centeredness and away from your own material gain.

Let's keep going. In the first chapter, Norman Greenbaum imagines going to "the place that's best." In the next chapter, John Lennon encourages the listener to consider a different viewpoint – maybe there is no "place that's best."

Section II

Our journey continues,
but we encounter
bewildering signs.
These songwriters
sow confusion
and disorient the travelers.

CHAPTER 4

"Imagine"

by John Lennon

WHERE WERE YOU on Sunday evening, February 9, 1964? If you were alive and living in the United States, you were probably one of the 73 million Americans in front of your TV set watching the Ed Sullivan Show. Why? Because this was the introduction of "the lads from Liverpool" to the U.S. audience. Recall the scene – young women and girls screaming hysterically, while The Beatles played this newfangled music, typically standing in their one spot wearing their jackets and ties, looking tidy with their "bowl" haircuts.

They played five songs that night – two different sets. Trivia question: What were the five songs? I'll give you a minute. Okay, time's up. "All My Loving," "Till There Was You," "She Loves You," "I Saw Her Standing There," and "I Want to Hold Your Hand."

Not all were enthralled. Here is Newsweek's review: "Visually, they are a nightmare. Musically, they are a near-disaster. Their lyrics punctuated by shouts of 'yeah, yeah, yeah.' The odds are they will fade away." [9] I wonder if the reviewer was related to one of those experts who predicted the internet would just be a passing fad.

The Beatles

If you have been living in a cave on a Pacific island since the end of World War II, it's possible you have not heard of John Lennon and The Beatles. They are widely regarded as the most influential band of all time. They are the biggest selling band of all time, having sold over 500 million records.

Just about every act of theirs has been chronicled and captured on film and every word parsed. There is no need for me to replay the entire story of the Beatles here. I'll just offer a few nuggets. Living in Liverpool, England, Lennon met Paul McCartney in 1957; McCartney joined Lennon's band "The Quarrymen" soon after. A year later, George Harrison, at the age of 14, joined. Ringo Starr came on the scene in 1962.

In a 1987 interview, McCartney said: "We all looked up to John. He was older and very much the leader. He was the quickest wit and the smartest." [10]

Their years of touring took them all over the world – starting in Hamburg, Germany and ending on the rooftop of their Apple Corps headquarters in London. Their last "official" concert was on August 29, 1966, at Candlestick Park in San Francisco. They played to an audience of 25,000 while 7,000 tickets were unsold. Sure, Candlestick is windy but come on – the Beatles last concert; put on a sweater and a windbreaker.

Their globetrotting also took them to India as part of a spiritual journey prompted by Lennon and Harrison.

The Beatles broke up near the end of 1969. I'm not about to weigh in on who, how or why they split at the height of their popularity. I just know that I and many millions of others have enjoyed their music from "Meet the Beatles" to "Let It Be."

John Lennon

The context of his years with The Beatles is obviously a huge part of appreciating Lennon's life. But we will now turn our attention to focus exclusively on Lennon as he, along with his wife Yoko Ono, wrote the song that is the subject of this chapter.

He was born on October 9, 1940, in Liverpool. His father was a merchant seaman who was often away. While he was gone, Lennon's mother had a child with another man. When his father returned, they had a custody battle. They both lost. So, at the age of 5, Lennon's aunt took custody of him.

Rebellion began early. He was quoted: "I was the one whose all other boys' parents, including Paul's father, would say 'keep away from him.'" [11]

Lennon's life took another tragic turn when he was 18 and learned that his mother, Julia, was struck and killed by a car while she was walking home.

Lennon was raised an Anglican by his aunt. He attended Liverpool College of Art but dropped out to pursue his rock & roll dream.

He was married to Cynthia Powell from 1962 to 1968. They had a son, Julian (of Hey Jude fame). In 1969, Lennon married Yoko Ono, and they had a son, Sean.

They were living in New York when Lennon was assassinated on December 8, 1980, outside the Dakota Hotel by a so-called fan.

Lennon was a prolific songwriter with the Beatles, teaming up primarily with McCartney, as well as during "The 70's" when he wrote alone and with Yoko. He is credited with writing or co-writing 25 number one singles.

Background of "Imagine"

Poems from Yoko's book "Grapefruit" inspired Lennon to write the lyrics for "Imagine." She described the lyrics as just what Lennon believed – we are all one country, one world, one people. The song encourages its listeners to imagine no heaven, no countries and no possessions. The opening lines: "Imagine there's no heaven; it's easy if you try." We can work toward the dream of unity by eliminating, or at least minimizing, what divides us.

Unity. The irony is that in a very different context, Revelation 7:9 echoes a similar sentiment – "a great multitude from every nation, all tribes, peoples and tongues" worshipping the Lord together. While Lennon and Yoko imagine no Heaven as one of the keys to world unity, the Bible gives this picture of true unity *in* Heaven.

"Imagine," which was recorded on May 27, 1971, still captivates the world. [12] More than 200 artists have performed or covered the song. On October 9, 1990, on what would have been Lennon's 50th birthday, more than 1 billion people listened to a broadcast of the song. It was featured at the closing ceremony of the 2012 Summer Olympics in London. "Imagine" has been played before the New Year's Eve ball drop at Time Square. Understandable – the song can inspire us to work toward a world free of the things that divide us.

A Personal Note

I believe there can be a kernel of usefulness in imagining no Heaven. At least, thought is being given as to whether or not there is an after-life.

Lennon and Yoko imagine a utopian world, free of things that divide us – religion, nationalism, materialism. Actually, there was once a utopian world. No, not Camelot. It was called Eden. God, in His infinite wisdom, will one day restore Eden. The irony of the opening line of the song is the view that when you die, that's the end versus the biblical promise of an eternal utopia with our Creator.

Heaven *is* a mystery and therefore calls for imagination. Lennon and Yoko used theirs to draw one conclusion. I use my imagination, bolstered by the Word of my Creator, to draw the opposite conclusion.

When I think about Heaven, I don't see myself sitting on a cloud playing a harp. Instead, I imagine reuniting with my father and other family and friends, meeting earlier generations of family members, conversing with biblical characters, getting answers to perplexing questions, learning how I may have impacted people without being aware, and ultimately, meeting my Maker and my Lord. And that's just my limited, finite mind. I believe Heaven is going to reflect God's creative power in ways exponentially beyond what I can conceive.

I love to imagine Heaven. Having an eternal perspective is foundational for my faith. So, if I have that perspective, it makes sense to me to meditate on what the next chapter of my life might look like.

What Does the Bible Say?

A lot! In the New Testament, there are more than 350 verses on Heaven. Jesus mentions Heaven 70 times in the book of Matthew alone. The topic of Heaven spans all of scripture – from the first chapter of Genesis to the last chapter of Revelation. And yet, Heaven remains a mystery.

It is not the scope of this chapter to dive in and try to understand and / or prove Heaven and Hell. The reference in the first stanza to "imagining no Heaven" reflects a skepticism about an afterlife, a disbelief in eternity.

Naturally, this runs counter to Scripture. Ecclesiastes 3:11 reminds us that God, our Creator, has "set eternity in the heart of man." The disbelief also runs counter to our own intuition.

This world is not fair. Rich, cruel, powerful people seem to get away with their actions and live extravagantly, often on the backs of the poor. We see this kind of injustice every day and wonder if it will ever be rectified. It will. God is a Righteous Judge (Psalm 7:11). This is the message of Psalm 73, where the author laments the world's unfairness. The pivot point of the chapter is verse 17 – "Until I came into the sanctuary of God." And regained eternal perspective – confident that the evil rulers of his day would receive God's justice throughout eternity, just as we can count on His justice toward the evil, unrepentant men and women of modern times, those who enslave and oppress the least fortunate among us. Scripture and intuition are aligned.

The Bible tells us several things about what Heaven will be like for those who choose to believe the words of Jesus and act on them. John 14:2 reads: "In My Father's house are many rooms; if it were not so, I would have told you; for I go to prepare a place for you." Here's the extent of my imagination. So, for all eternity, I get a room? Sounds a little claustrophobic. How big will my room be? Will the bed be comfortable? Will I get ESPN? Who will my neighbors be? I hope I like them. And that they keep their place clean and are not noisy. I can poke fun at my finite mind. I suspect that my "room" in Heaven will not just be a penthouse with 24-hour room service and a great view, but it will redefine "room" so far beyond the best I can conceive.

In a similar vein, when I read Revelation, I get the sense that my daily activity will simply be chanting words and singing songs of praise to my Creator and my Lord. Not saying they don't deserve it; just seems like after 1,000 days or so, it might get a little old. Again, I laugh at my own limited mind. Joining other believers in praise, being present at the wedding feast talked about in Revelation 19 will far surpass my wildest dreams.

Using the word "imagine," the Christian band Mercy Me takes us on an uplifting journey.

"I Can Only Imagine" – Mercy Me [13]

While Lennon and Yoko encouraged listeners to imagine no Heaven or Hell, but simply a utopian earth free of divisiveness, Bart Millard of Mercy Me used his creativity to raise our view of Heaven and prompt our own meditation on what it will be like. His opening lyrics:

> I can only imagine
> What it will be like
> When I walk by Your side

I can only imagine
What my eyes would see
When Your face is before me

Surrounded by Your glory
What will my heart feel?
Will I dance for You Jesus
Or in awe of You be still? [14]

In the movie "I Can Only Imagine," we learn that Millard's dad was abusive. Lennon's dad abandoned him. I find it illuminating to trace the different paths their lives took in response to unfit fathers. Contrast Millard's song about Heaven to Lennon's. Both are beautiful melodies; but Millard's lyrics alone contain eternal truth.

Back to Lennon's "Imagine" – Thoughts on the Last Stanza

(Note: I am jumping past the second stanza of the song, "imagining no countries," simply because I didn't make a connection to spiritual matters, good or bad. Looking back through history, many nations' boundaries were created artificially. Maps were redrawn after wars, sowing the seeds of future conflict. Imagining no countries in today's world seems an exercise in futility, but one can at least understand the sentiment behind it.)

However, the third stanza, "imagining no possessions," does have spiritual implications. I suspect what Lennon meant by "no possessions" is a world with a more equitable distribution of wealth, instead of a world with the rich "haves" and the poor "have nots." One could say this sounds like socialism. Perhaps. It also sounds like Acts 2:44-45 describing the early church:

> "And all those who had believed were together, and
> had all things in common, and they began selling
> their property and possessions, and were sharing
> them with all, as anyone might have need."

This sacrificial life had its roots in Jesus's teachings. In Matthew 16:26, He asks: "For what will a man be profited if he gains the whole world, and forfeits his soul?" This troubling question hangs in the air today just like it did 2,000 years ago.

Jesus gets more personal with the rich young ruler (Mark 10:17-27), who wants to know what he must do to inherit eternal life. Jesus reminds him of the commandments, which he claims to have kept. Then Jesus challenges him: "Go and sell all you possess and give it to the poor." Verse 22 reads: "At these words, his face fell, and he went away grieved, for he was one who owned much property."

Jesus not only taught about sharing our wealth with the poor, but he lived a life of material poverty. He was homeless. In Matthew 8:20, He says: "The foxes have holes and the birds of the air have nests, but the Son of Man has nowhere to lay His head."

Jesus exemplified the life imagined in the third stanza of Lennon's song.

A Final Word

In an odd way, Lennon and Yoko wanted what Christians want – utopia. They dreamed of seeing it happen on earth strictly through the efforts of mankind, which time and again produces disappointment as human sinfulness, greed, and pride undermine progress.

On the other hand, utopia can be realized as we pass from this life to the next. The best-known verse in the Bible, John 3:16, tells us: "For God so loved the world, that He gave His only Son, that whoever believes in Him shall not perish, but have eternal life." Yes, John, there is a utopia. It's called Heaven.

CHAPTER 5

"Money"

by Pink Floyd

IN THE 1970S sitcom "All in the Family," Archie Bunker often misquotes or mischaracterizes what's in the Bible, usually to bolster an argument he is having with his son-in-law, "Meathead." A few of the more memorable: [15]

- "Like the good book says, he who is without sin … be the rolling stone."
- "God don't make no mistakes; that's how he got to be God."
- "All these old Bible people always eating meat after they found out eating apples was wrong."

These were humorous. Other mischaracterizations are more misleading. John 1:1 reads: "In the beginning was the

Word (Jesus), and the Word was with God, and the Word was God." The Jehovah's Witness Bible closes that verse with: "the Word was a god." Intent to mislead? The addition of the article "a" undermines the foundation of the Christian faith – that Jesus was fully God and fully man.

In their song "Money," Pink Floyd was not being humorous or misleading, but they did misquote the Bible on the topic of money, as many do. Pink Floyd would likely not have a clue as to why any of the lyrics of any of their songs would be referenced in a book about Jesus and rock & roll.

This chapter of the book is a little different from the first four. Each of the others knew they were writing about something that had spiritual overtones – lighthearted or otherwise.

Background on Pink Floyd, "The Dark Side of the Moon" and the song "Money"

Pink Floyd started out in London in 1965. (Five chapters in, you can see why it was called "the British Invasion.") Syd Barrett came up with the name of the band on the spur of the moment by combining the names of two blues musicians – Pink Anderson and Floyd Council. Guitarist David Gilmour and Bassist Roger Waters were the band's mainstays. Conflict among the band members was the norm.

Conflict did not impede their creative genius, as reflected in their iconic album "Dark Side of the Moon." Their 8th album, it was recorded between May 1972 and

January 1973; released on March 1, 1973, at Abbey Road Studios. It is the world's 4th best-selling album of all-time.

The "dark side" was an allusion to lunacy rather than astronomy. The album explored themes such as conflict, greed, time, death and mental illness.

The song "Money," the first song on the back side, was released on May 7, 1973. It was their first major hit in the U.S. While it mocked greed and consumerism, it is interesting that Waters later remarked: "I have to decide whether I am a socialist or not. I'm still keen on a general welfare society, but I became a capitalist. I remember coveting a Bentley like crazy." [16]

"Money"– The Lyric (singular)

Unlike the other songs we have highlighted so far, most of the lyrics of "Money" are not relevant in terms of relating them to spiritual matters. Actually, none are, except: "Money, so they say, is the root of all evil today."

I wonder who "they" is and where they first got this notion. I submit that without necessarily being aware, they got it from the Bible: I Timothy 6:10 reads: "For the love of money is the root of all sorts of evil."

Only what "they" say is not what the Bible says, which is the purpose of including this song in a book entitled "Rock & Roll and the Rock of Ages."

Here is our opportunity to provide clarification.

So, What Does the Bible Say About Money? (Not Archie Bunker's Bible; THE Bible)

A lot. Over 2,000 verses, Old and New Testament, mention money. Over 25% of Jesus's parables deal with money.

It's clear that money in and of itself is not evil. In Jesus's time, as in ours, some wealthy people used their riches wisely – to bless others. Abraham was a wealthy man and God told him in Genesis 12:2 "I will bless you so you shall be a blessing."

It seems like the biblical view of money can be captured in two words: stewardship and idolatry. In the Sermon on the Mount, Jesus says (Matthew 6:20-21): "But lay up for yourselves treasures in Heaven, where neither moth nor rust destroys, and where thieves do not break in or steal; for where your treasure is, there will your heart be also." Three verses later: "No one can serve two masters, for either he will hate the one and love the other, or he will hold to one and despise the other. You cannot serve God and mammon (money)." In an earlier chapter of this book, we saw that the rich young ruler could not walk away from his riches to follow Jesus. This is idolatry. This is "the love of money." Hebrews 13:5 drives home the point: "Let your character be free from the love of money."

Those who have been blessed with wealth face the challenge of good stewardship. In Matthew 19:24, Jesus tells His disciples that "it is easier for a camel to go through the eye of a needle than for a rich man to enter the kingdom of God." When the disciples question Him about this statement, He explains that nothing is impossible for God. The point is that wealthy people may be more likely to be distracted by things of the world and by the desire to amass more riches. Ecclesiastes 5:10 tells us: "Whoever loves money never has enough."

But everyone, wealthy or not, is responsible for being a faithful steward. One shining example of good stewardship in the Bible is the widow in Luke 21:1-4, who puts two small copper coins in the offering plate. Jesus affirms her this way: "Truly, I say to you, this poor widow put in more than all of them. For they out of their surplus put into the offering, but she out of her poverty put in all that she had to live on."

Good stewardship starts with the recognition that everything belongs to God. Psalm 50:10 reminds us that God says, "Every beast of the field is Mine, the cattle on a thousand hills."

Stewardship runs deeper than that. It is a recognition that we are not our own. We find that in I Corinthians 6:19-20 – "you are not your own; you have been bought with a price." We are called to be good stewards of the lives God has given us, of the children He may have blessed us with, and of any material wealth that we have received.

Job recognized this. He was a very wealthy man, but God allowed his wealth to vanish. Rather than lash out against God, he praised Him: "The Lord gave, and the Lord has taken away. Blessed be the name of the Lord" (Job 1:21).

As Paul said in Philippians 4:11-12, "I have learned to be content in whatever circumstances I am. I know how to get along with humble means, and I also know how to live in prosperity." Money was not an idol for Job or Paul; neither exhibited the love of money. Job's fortunes were restored, while Paul was on the run most of his life. I suspect that, as a tentmaker, he did not have a large retirement account.

The Bible reminds us that "It is more blessed to give than to receive" (Acts 20:35). Proverbs 19:17 echoes this sentiment: "He who is gracious to a poor man lends to the Lord, and He will repay him for his good deed."

On the other hand, several verses serve as a warning against greed. One example among many is found in Proverbs 21:13, "He who shuts his ear to the cry of the poor will also cry himself and not be answered." Just preceding the "love of money" reference in I Timothy 6 is verse 9, which reads: "Those who want to get rich fall into temptation and a trap and into many foolish and harmful desires that plunge people into ruin and destruction." Greed is linked to justice – God's righteous justice. The greedy will get their due – whether in this life or the next.

A Final Word

Even though Pink Floyd misquoted the Bible, their mockery of materialism and greed is consistent with the biblical exhortation to avoid greed and embrace generosity. "God loves a cheerful giver" (I Corinthians 9:7).

Thank you, Pink Floyd, for at least shining a spotlight on the futility of materialism and a misguided, insatiable quest for more and more. The logical conclusion then, consistent with Scripture, is that a fulfilled life is a product of generosity and contentment and gratitude for what we have been blessed with, as well as responding to the call to be faithful stewards.

CHAPTER 6

"My Sweet Lord"

by George Harrison

WHEN I WAS much younger, I conducted a very unscientific survey of teenage girls who loved the Beatles. Question: Who was your favorite Beatle? George Harrison won in a landslide. Not sure why. He was known as "the quiet Beatle." He was the youngest. Later, we learn he had a big heart. I guess he was considered handsome. Perhaps the main reason is because young women grew tired of naming Paul, John or even Ringo as their favorite. That left George.

Background on George Harrison

As noted in the chapter on Lennon's "Imagine," if you are from another planet, it's possible you are not familiar with the Beatles. So much has been written about their success, their relationships, their journey that it would be redundant to replay it here.

On the other hand, devoting more space to the life of George Harrison, especially his search for spiritual meaning, is important as it provides context for his songwriting throughout his solo career, most notably the song we are examining in this chapter, "My Sweet Lord."

His Personal Life

Harrison was born on February 25, 1943, in Liverpool, the youngest of four children. He met Paul McCartney on a school bus at the age of 14. They attended the Liverpool Institute for High School Boys. A year later, Harrison auditioned for McCartney and Lennon's group, the Quarrymen. Lennon thought he was too young, but a second audition convinced him otherwise.

Harrison married Pattie Boyd in 1966; they divorced in 1977. A year later, he married Olivia Arias, and they had a son, Dhani.

Harrison's music career and spiritual journey were cut short as he lost his battle with cancer and died on November 29, 2001, in Beverly Hills.

He was inducted into the Rock & Roll Hall of Fame in 1988 as a member of the Beatles and again in 2004 (posthumously) for his solo career. He was recognized in 2015 with a Grammy Lifetime Achievement Award.

His Music Career

Harrison played lead guitar for the Beatles. The sheer volume, and of course quality, of songs written by Lennon and McCartney thrust Harrison's own songwriting skills into the background. However, most Beatles' albums from 1965 onward contained at least two songs he wrote, most memorably "Something" and "Here Comes the Sun" on the Abbey Road album and "While My Guitar Gently Weeps" on the White album. In fact, "Something" became the second most covered Beatles song after "Yesterday."

As the 60's came to a close, Harrison grew more frustrated with what he viewed as Lennon and McCartney's domination. The drifting apart had begun earlier as Harrison learned to play the sitar and immersed himself in Indian music with his friend, Ravi Shankar. His last recording session with the Beatles was January 4, 1970.

Harrison immediately embarked on his solo career. His elite status as a songwriter was validated with the first album he released, "All Things Must Pass," where the song that is the subject of this chapter appears.

In 1971, he gathered rock music royalty together for two nights in sold-out Madison Square Garden for "The Concert for Bangladesh" to raise money for the destitute of that poverty-stricken, war-torn nation. Harrison's solo career continued to reflect his political activism, such as support for the civil rights movement, as well as his humanitarianism, promoting his wife Olivia's work on behalf of Romanian orphans left abandoned following the fall of Communism.

His Spiritual Journey

It appears that two factors around 1966-67 served as catalysts for his spiritual exploration. One was his use of LSD. In a 1977 interview, he recalled: "The first time I had acid, it just opened up something in my head that was inside of me and I realized a lot of things.... From the moment I had that, I wanted to have it all the time – these things about the yogis and the Himalayas and Ravi's music." [17]

The second factor, obviously intertwined, began with the first trip he and Pattie Boyd took to India in 1966, where he studied sitar with Shankar and visited several holy Hindu sites. In 1968, he returned to India to study meditation with Maharishi Mahesh Yogi.

As he was captivated by Indian philosophy, culture and religion, he became enmeshed in the Hare Krishna Movement. Similar to his reflection about his use of LSD, in referring to the Hare Krishna chant, Harrison said: "The more I do it, I find the harder it is to stop, and I don't want to lose the feeling it gives me. For example, once I chanted the Hare Krishna mantra all the way from France to Portugal. I drove for about twenty-three hours and chanted all the way." [18]

George Harrison – a heart for the marginalized and a desire to find spiritual meaning throughout his adult life.

Background on "My Sweet Lord"

The song was inspired by the Edwin Hawkins Singers' gospel hit "Oh Happy Day." "My Sweet Lord" was the first number one hit by an ex-Beatle. Harrison began writing it in December 1969 in Copenhagen and completed it with Billy Preston when they returned to London.

He wrote the song in praise of the Hindu god Krishna. The lyrics are directed at the notion of one god who pervades everything, is everywhere, all-knowing and all-powerful, and transcends time and space. Harrison wanted to fuse the messages of the major religions and suggested that all Christians, Hindus, Jews, Muslims, Buddhists and others can address our gods in the same way, using the phrase "My Sweet Lord."

The familiar lyrics begin with "My Sweet Lord, I really want to see you, I want to be with you, I really want to know you, I really want to go with you, Lord." [19] These lines are repeated once, punctuated with a few "Hallelujahs," which is an expression of worship and praise for the Lord.

The song winds down, interspersing "my sweet Lord" with multiple Hallelujahs, Hare Krishnas and other references to Hindu deities. The Hare Krishna chant can mean: Krishna, the Hindu god of love, come and take over the chariot (my life) on the battlefield.

The song reflects Harrison's view of the spiritual world, captured in this quote: "All religions are branches of one big tree. It doesn't matter what you call him as long as you call." [20]

What Does the Bible Say?

We'll return to that last quote. But first, let's acknowledge Harrison's desire to see the Lord, to be with the Lord, and especially to know the Lord.

While I commend his desire, my heart aches for him and others who seek unknowable gods. The God of the Bible wants to be known.

The Inscription

In the Sermon on Mars Hill, the Apostle Paul in Acts 17:22-25 makes the case for a knowable God: "Men of Athens, I observe that you are very religious in all respects. For while I was passing through and examining the objects of your worship, I also found an altar with this inscription 'TO AN UNKNOWN GOD.' What therefore you worship in ignorance, this I proclaim to you. (Ed. Note: Paul didn't sugarcoat his message.) The God who made the world and all things in it, since He is Lord of Heaven and Earth, does not dwell in temples made with hands; neither is He served by human hands, as though He needed anything, since He Himself gives to all life and breath and all things."

In verse 27, Paul goes on to say: "that they seek God, if perhaps they might grope for Him and find Him, though He is not far from each one of us."

In Jeremiah 9:24, we are exhorted to: "Let him who boasts boast of this, that he understands and knows Me, that I am the Lord who exercises lovingkindness, justice and righteousness on earth."

J.I. Packer's book "Knowing God" [21] draws a distinction between knowing about God and knowing God, the latter "a relationship calculated to thrill a man's heart." Packer devotes a chapter to each of God's primary attributes, such as lovingkindness, justice and righteousness, noted in the Jeremiah 9 verse above, to introduce the reader to the character of God.

As Packer points out, the character of God is clearly and ultimately revealed in His Son, who walked the earth for 33 years and exhibited the identical character as His Father. Jesus, who can be known as an historical figure through the Gospels, is the bridge to knowing God, the Father.

Every day, He stands at the door (of our hearts) and knocks (Revelation 3:20). He wants to be known. Those who let Him in experience the love of the Father, a love described so movingly in the parable of the Prodigal Son (Luke 15:11-32). The rebellious, yet repentant, son returns sheepishly to his home, hoping for some small measure of forgiveness. Instead, his father runs to meet him with outstretched arms, embracing him and welcoming him home. In the same way, God, the Father, offers forgiveness and rushes toward each one of us with exuberance, seeking to bring us into His family.

While Harrison refers to really wanting to know God but not sure how or who the true God is, I encourage you to accept that the God of the Bible is the true God; that He wants to be known; that He wants to enjoy a relationship with His creation; and that He seeks you and me as adopted brothers and sisters of His only begotten Son, Jesus.

The Tree and Its Branches

Let's return to Harrison's comment that "All religions are branches of one big tree." That is a popular and understandable notion. However, it is wholly inconsistent with the Bible. Jesus states it plainly in John 14:6, "I am the way and the truth and the life; no one comes to the Father, but through Me." Other major religions may attempt to graft Jesus into their narratives, but the Christian faith is clear that He was more than simply a good teacher. He was, and is, the Son of God.

Jesus knew the hearts of men, that some would use the word "Lord," but misappropriate it. In Matthew 7:21-23, He says: "Not everyone who says to Me, 'Lord, Lord,' will enter the Kingdom of Heaven, but he who does the will of My Father will enter. Many will say to Me on that day, 'Lord, Lord.' I will then declare to them, 'I never knew you; depart from Me.'"

Attempting to merge the world's major religions ("one tree; many branches"), as the song "My Sweet Lord" does, can be puzzling for those genuinely searching for truth.

The Bible mentions trees and branches several times. Genesis 2:9 is the first of multiple references to the Tree of Life, which represents the eternal life that God wishes to give each one of us, starting the day we truly believe in Him. The last chapter of the last book of the Bible, Revelation 22, makes two references to the Tree of Life, encouraging those who have repented and turned to the Lord that they have "the right to the Tree of Life." This thread runs through the Bible from the beginning to the end.

Branches come into play in John 15:5, where Jesus says: "I am the vine; you are the branches; he who abides in Me and I in him, he bears much fruit." Abide in Him; rest in Him; know Him. He wants to be known.

These are the tree and branch metaphors that I choose to base my life on.

Personal Reflection

As Harrison seemed to be on a genuine quest for truth and spirituality, I likewise have been on a spiritual journey, albeit arriving at a profoundly different conclusion from Harrison.

Ministry at the United Nations

When I worked in New York, I had the privilege of serving on the Board of the Christian Mission to the United Nations Community. In that capacity, I had the opportunity to meet one-on-one with Ambassadors and other diplomats from all over the world. I was amazed at their degree of openness as we shared our views on spiritual matters. Virtually every conversation was marked by mutual respect and civility and a desire to understand each other.

Confession: With the benefit of hindsight, I can see that I may have unintentionally upheld Harrison's "all branches of one tree" metaphor in an attempt to build common ground, especially with the Muslim delegates to the UN, using Abraham as the focal point. Fortunately, before I got too far down the road with this thought, the realization struck me that I was watering down my own faith. I do serve the God of Abraham, but as revealed in Jesus and no other, which drew a clear line of demarcation between me and my Muslim friends. Despite our different beliefs, the mutual respect and attempt to understand the other never wavered.

Exclusivity

Christians oftentimes encounter backlash from what is viewed as the exclusivity of our faith. We claim there is one way to God, the Father, and that's through Jesus Christ, His Son, as stated in John 14:6.

But it's not exclusive. All are welcome, as the invitation in Matthew 11:28 expresses: "Come to Me, all who are weary and heavy-laden and I will give you rest." Revelation 7:9 describes the joyous scene in Heaven, where there will be "a great multitude from every nation and all tribes and peoples and tongues."

And yet, I acknowledge a type of exclusivity of the Christian faith. I believe I'm right that Jesus is the only way to God and that religions that suggest otherwise are wrong. That may sound harsh or arrogant, but it's really not. I'm taking a risk; I'm betting my life on a relationship with an unseen God and a man who was last seen on the outskirts of Jerusalem 2,000 years ago.

If I'm wrong and Muhammad or Krishna or Buddha or a combination of all, as Harrison espoused, are the true god(s), then I'm prepared to accept the consequences – in eternity or as my life comes to a close and I return to dust.

A Final Word

This chapter was harder to write than the others. Each of the other artists wrote a song and I could offer my thoughts based solely on their lyrics seen through my Christian world view. But in the case of Harrison and "My Sweet Lord," the song captures the essence of his heart and soul. Throughout this book, I have focused on lyrics without, I hope, a trace of judging the songwriter's heart.

I appreciate Harrison's journey – his search for spiritual enlightenment. However, it seems to me that he arrived at the wrong destination. Jesus leads me on my journey, and He is my destination.

Jesus is My Sweet Lord.

HOMESTRETCH

THE LAST THREE chapters ("Imagine," "Money," and "My Sweet Lord") represent a detour as we head toward the homestretch. In the first three chapters, we saw that "you gotta have a friend in Jesus," that he (Satan) "was around when Jesus had his moment of doubt and pain," and that "Oh Lord…", you can talk to Him and ask Him for anything.

While remaining attuned to the spiritual world, these last three chapters have taken a different turn.

- Imagining there's no Heaven could imply that it's just as easy to imagine there is. The Bible tells us there is, but certainly doesn't clear up all the mystery around Heaven. That's why I chose to include Mercy Me's "I Can Only Imagine" as a sort of counterweight to Lennon's misguided suggestion wrapped in a beautiful melody.

- "Money" was an odd song to include, but the intent was to showcase how Scripture can be slightly misquoted and change the meaning entirely. Wealth *is* frequently misused, but often generosity prevails. Money is not the root of all evil, as the song says. The love of money is the root of all evil, as the Bible says.

- "My Sweet Lord" attempts to placate all its listeners with the notion that "all religions are branches of the same tree." Harrison chose to call out to Krishna as his god. I believe this is akin to the prophets of Baal calling to their god as a sort of competition with Elijah calling on his God to determine who the true God was (and is). They called, but "no one answered." Elijah suggests "perhaps he is on a journey or asleep." The God of the Bible never sleeps, always listens and answers in *His* perfect timing.

The detour was designed so that the confusion could be exposed.

We now move to the last three songs, which provide a glimpse of the tender, compassionate and personal Jesus.

Section III

Our journey takes us to the summit, where we have a clear and exhilarating view. These songwriters hit the target. Jesus - our Friend, our Guide, our Destination.

CHAPTER 7

"Mrs. Robinson"

by Simon and Garfunkel

"PLASTICS" – WITH this one word, movie buffs of all ages can identify the movie – "The Graduate." [22] Just about as well-known is the sentence: "Mrs. Robinson, I think you're trying to seduce me." She was and she did.

The Movie

Released on December 21, 1967, "The Graduate" was a movie that defined a generation and spotlighted the generation gap. Ben, played by Dustin Hoffman, was a recent college graduate who moved back into his parents' house in Pasadena, California, having no idea what he wanted to do with his life. The advice from well-meaning friends of his parents ("one word – plastics") further alienated him away from a typical career path.

At the same time, the wife of his father's law partner, Mrs. Robinson (played by Anne Bancroft), was bored with her life and with her marriage. The intersection of Ben's aimlessness and Mrs. Robinson's boredom led to the affair.

In the meantime, Ben falls for Mrs. Robinson's daughter, Elaine (played by Katharine Ross). As her wedding ceremony to be married to Carl is about to begin, Ben shows up in time to scream "Elaine" from the back of the church. She turns around, leaves with Ben, and let's assume they lived happily ever after.

A few interesting anecdotes related to the movie:

- Hoffman was supposedly paid $20,000 for his role in the film. A pretty good return on investment for the producers.
- Robert Redford was considered for the part of Ben, but the Director, Mike Nichols, concluded he would not be convincing as a sexually awkward young man.
- Another person considered but not chosen for an important role, Ben's father, went on to greater fame – Ronald Reagan.

For that matter, so did Simon and Garfunkel.

Background on the Duo

Paul Simon was born on October 13, 1941, in Newark, New Jersey to parents of Hungarian-Jewish descent. When he was four, his family moved to Queens, New York. Art Garfunkel was born on November 5, 1941, in Queens to parents of Romanian-Jewish descent. Simon and Garfunkel met in the 6th grade where they both had roles in the school play, "Alice in Wonderland."

Together, they made five studio albums and a number of live albums. They broke up in 1970, in part, because Garfunkel wanted to pursue an acting career alongside their concert tour schedule.

They reunited off and on, most memorably at a 1981 Concert in Central Park. They were inducted into the Rock & Roll Hall of Fame in 1990, and in 2003 received the Grammy Lifetime Achievement Award.

Paul Simon

As a young boy, Simon played baseball and stickball and became a lifelong New York Yankees fan. He graduated from Queens College in 1963. He and Garfunkel then released their first album, "Wednesday Morning, 3:00 A.M," which was initially a failure. Simon moved to London in 1965 but soon returned and he and Garfunkel completed four albums until they parted ways in 1970. That year, Simon taught songwriting at New York University. In a 2011 interview with music journalist Tom Moon, he discussed the basic themes in his songwriting: love, family and social commentary, as well as messages of religion, spirituality and God. Simon was inducted into the Rock & Roll Hall of Fame in 2001 for his solo career. He played his final concert in Queens on September 22, 2018.

Another facet of Simon's career resulted from his friendship with Lorne Michaels, the creator of Saturday Night Live. Simon has appeared on the show 14 times. He hosted the second show on October 18, 1975. A little over a year later, he teamed up on SNL with George Harrison as they sung "Here Comes the Sun" and "Homeward Bound." Oh, to be in the audience that night.

Art Garfunkel

Garfunkel grew up with two brothers, a mother who was a homemaker, and a father who was a traveling salesman. When he was young, he often sang in the synagogue. Garfunkel earned a Bachelor of Arts degree in History and a Master of Arts in Mathematics Education from Columbia University. Like Simon, he was an avid baseball fan. However, his allegiance was to the Philadelphia Phillies. Maybe that's why they broke up!

Garfunkel was a poet, an actor and a singer, but not a songwriter. Simon's mother told her son: "You have a good voice, Paul, but Artie has a fine voice." [23] Simon wrote the songs that made them both household names.

So now we turn to one of the most famous songs Simon wrote, "Mrs. Robinson," the subject of this chapter.

Background on "Mrs. Robinson" (The Song)

Simon had been working on a song called "Mrs. Roosevelt." He explained that it was not for the movie; it was about nostalgia for times past, exemplified by Eleanor Roosevelt and Joe DiMaggio. The song was released on April 5, 1968, more than three months after "The Graduate" first appeared in movie theaters. Prior to the movie's release, Simon agreed to change the name of the song to Mrs. Robinson at the request of Mike Nichols. The movie contained only fragments of the song. Nonetheless, the movie provides important context for purposes of this chapter.

As a refresher, the chorus of the song is: "And here's to you, Mrs. Robinson, Jesus loves you more than you will know. God bless you please, Mrs. Robinson, Heaven holds a place for those who pray." The last chorus and perhaps the best-known lyric is: "Where have you gone, Joe DiMaggio? One nation turns its lonely eyes to you." [24]

What Does the Bible Say?

Fans of the New York Yankees might be surprised to learn that Joe DiMaggio is not mentioned in the Bible. However, he is remembered for the grace with which he patrolled center field and handled the media glare off the field. Probably an overreach to link Joltin' Joe's grace with the grace that permeates the Bible. Internet research yields interesting background on the DiMaggio line, but virtually nothing related to the lyrics about Jesus and Heaven.

From the Gospel of John

Maybe we can change that. Let's start with "Jesus loves you more than you will know." Perhaps the best-known verse in the Bible is John 3:16, "For God so loved the world, that He gave His only Son, that whosoever believes in Him will not perish but have eternal life."

The very next verse reads: "For God did not send the Son into the world to judge the world, but that the world might be saved through Him."

One of the most poignant examples of Jesus not exhibiting judgment is found in John 8 where the Pharisees brought to Jesus a woman caught in the act of adultery. In an effort to trap Him, they asked how He would handle this situation. He ignored them, but they persisted. So He responded, "He who is without sin, let him be the first to cast a stone." The Pharisees departed and He was left alone with the woman. He asked: "Did no one condemn you?" She responded: "No one, Lord." Jesus said: "Then neither do I condemn you."

Imagine what the woman experienced at that moment – how overwhelmed with relief and joy she must have felt by the forgiveness Jesus proclaimed. Jesus came into the world to bring light into the darkness, to show unconditional love, to exhibit compassion and to extend forgiveness.

Mrs. Robinson was in the same boat as the adulterous woman from 2000 years ago. No wonder the song's opening line was: "Jesus loves you more than you will know," exemplified by His forgiveness rather than condemnation.

The woman caught in adultery needed forgiveness; Mrs. Robinson needed forgiveness; you and I need forgiveness – a forgiveness that takes on its deepest meaning when it comes from the Son of God.

Jesus and Women

It's not a surprise that Jesus would exhibit such compassion to this woman. There are numerous examples in the Gospels of His tender love for women.

Let's consider the status of women in the first century, especially within the Jewish community. Men were not allowed to greet women in public. Some Jewish writers taught that women should never leave the home except to go to the synagogue. Rabbi Eliezer, a first-century teacher, is noted for saying: "Rather should the word of the Torah be burned than entrusted to a woman."

Against this backdrop is the radical nature of Jesus's interactions with women. The Gospel writers include several accounts of His dialogues with women – some seeking to be healed, some having just been healed, others such as Mary, the sister of Lazarus, learning from Jesus.

In the 4th chapter of the Book of John we find a beautiful exchange that in a simple way captures the essence of the Christian faith. Jesus is thirsty and asks a Samaritan woman to draw water for Him. Jews were not supposed to interact with Samaritans, much less a Samaritan woman, but Jesus does.

In the 10th verse, Jesus refers to living water. Naturally, the woman is confused. Verse 14 reads: "Whoever drinks of the water that I give shall never thirst; but the water that I shall give shall become in him (or her) a well of water springing up to eternal life." She responds: "Sir, give me this water." It feels like a cry of desperation.

She didn't know exactly what she was asking for, but she knew in her innermost being that she wanted the "living water" that only Jesus could provide. He still provides it today, and I believe most people intuitively realize they, too, want that living water.

Seduction

To close out this chapter, we'll take a detour from focusing on the song's lyrics and pull from the movie. Mrs. Robinson *was* trying (successfully it turns out) to seduce Ben.

The Bible has a lot to say about seduction. Not just sexual seduction, which is amply warned about in the Book of Proverbs but being seduced more broadly by what the world values. Wealth, status and appearance are a few of the avenues of seduction. The Bible counters each one with its focus on the heart and on an eternal perspective.

Wealth – The Bible reminds us to "lay up our treasures in Heaven; for where your treasure is, there will be your heart also" (Matthew 6:20-21). A little later in Matthew's Gospel (16:26), we are told: "For what will a man be profited if he gains the whole world and forfeits his soul?"

Status – Can be a powerful seducer. Yet Jesus turns the notion of status upside down. Again, in Matthew (5:5), we read "Blessed are the meek (the gentle), for they shall inherit the earth." To drive home the point, Matthew 20:16 says: "The first shall be last and the last first."

Appearance – Is another way the culture seduces us. Again, the Bible goes against the grain. I Samuel 16:7 tells us: "For the Lord sees not as man sees; man looks on the outward appearance, but the Lord looks on the heart."

What the world offers is fleeting, deceptive and seductive. What Jesus offers is the antidote - truth, grace and eternity with Him.

A Final Word

I trust that the woman caught in adultery who encountered the compassion of the living Lord turned her life around as a result. I pray that present-day Mrs. (and Mr.) Robinsons accept and internalize the forgiveness that Jesus provides and can therefore claim "Whom the Son sets free shall be free indeed."

CHAPTER 8

"Get Together"

by The Youngbloods

WHEN I RUN for political office (never), my platform may be vague and not terribly inspiring, but I have already picked out the theme song for my campaign – "Get Together" by The Youngbloods. [25] In this world of conflict, upheaval, divisiveness, and yes, hate, I'd like to think that the words of their chorus would resonate:

> Come on people now
> Smile on your brother
> Everybody get together
> Try to love another right now. [26]

Call me naïve, but I subscribe to the sentiment expressed in Proverbs 31:25 – we *can* "smile at the future." Seems to me it may begin with smiling on your brother and sister, as the song encourages us all.

While the chorus is beautiful – both lyrics and melody – in this chapter, we'll delve into the richness of each verse.

But first let's meet The Youngbloods and their leader, Jesse Colin Young.

Their Background

Young was born Perry Miller on November 22, 1941, in Queens, New York. When he began performing, he settled on the stage name, Jesse Colin Young. His mother was a violinist and a singer; his father was an accountant.

Young attended Phillips Academy in Andover, Massachusetts. He started off college life at Ohio State University and transferred to New York University in 1961. He began to perform in Greenwich Village, left college, and became a full-time musician. He married Suzi Young and they had two children – Juli and Cheyenne.

In 1965, he met Jerry Corbitt. They performed as a duo, taking the name "The Youngbloods." They added Joe Bauer as their drummer and Lowell ("Banana") Levinger who played guitar and piano. Young was the lead singer and played guitar and bass.

The group's only Top 40 hit was "Get Together." They produced four albums before they disbanded to pursue solo careers. Only Young had notable success as a solo artist.

He continued to perform until he was sidelined with a diagnosis of chronic Lyme disease in 2012. He retired from music at that time but returned four years later to perform with his son Tristan. Young and his second wife, Connie Darden, have two children – Tristan and Jazzie.

They lived in northern California until 1995 when a fire destroyed their home. That prompted Young to move the family to Hawaii, where he owned a coffee plantation. In 2006, they moved back to the mainland – to Aiken, South Carolina, his wife's hometown.

In interviews, Young mentions that he was a "born-again Christian" for a year when he was 16, but seems to downplay this later when he says, "The 60s were a time when we were open, but none of us was devoutly religious."

Over the years, he has been an activist for causes related to immigration, race, climate and nuclear disarmament.

Another artist with a heart for the downtrodden and a better planet while not offering much of a clue as to where he landed spiritually.

Background on the Song

To begin with, the Youngbloods didn't write it. Chet Powers did. However, Powers got arrested for drug possession and sold the rights to the song to RCA Records so he could afford an attorney to keep him out of prison.

Young and his bandmates, who had signed a recording contract with RCA, were rehearsing at Café au GoGo in

Greenwich Village when they first heard "Get Together." RCA released The Youngbloods' version of the song in 1967, but it only reached #62 on the charts. Their break came two years later. The song was used by the National Council of Christians and Jews as a "Brotherhood Week" promotion on TV and radio commercials. RCA agreed to re-release the song, and it became a Top 5 hit.

"Get Together" appeared on the soundtrack of the movie "Forrest Gump," as well as play on The Simpsons. The song has been covered by a diverse group ranging from Andy Williams and Louis Armstrong to the Dave Clark Five and Jefferson Airplane.

Years later, Young offered this recollection. "Just like in those movies about the Bible, the heavens opened, and my life changed. I knew that song was my path forward, not only as a musician, but as a human being."[27]

The Lyrics – The First Two Stanzas

Love is but a song we sing
Fear's the way we die
You can make the mountains ring
Or make the angels cry
Though the bird is on the wing
And you may not know why

Some may come and some may go
We will surely pass
When the one that left us here

Returns for us at last
We are but a moment's sunlight
Fading in the grass

In other chapters of this book, the lyrics are fairly clear and can be viewed against a biblical backdrop – consistent with or not.

However, the meaning of these words in "Get Together" is a little mysterious and therefore has to be inferred. It seems reasonable to conclude that there is spiritual meaning in the imagery, even biblical imagery, of these lyrics.

That's the way I interpret these words and using that as a base, we'll review the presumed meaning of each one as they stack up against what Scripture teaches.

What Does the Bible Say?

Love and Fear

Love is but a song we sing
Fear's the way we die.

The Bible says quite a lot about love and fear. These words are juxtaposed in a single verse, I John 4:18, "Perfect love casts out fear." Perfect love conquers fear. What is perfect love? None of us exhibit it; only Jesus did. But He encourages us to aspire to it in John 15:13, "Greater love has no one than this, that one lay down his life for his friends."

The command to "love one another" appears 11 times in the Bible. "Fear not" is found 25 times, while its companion phrase "Do not be afraid" appears over 300 times.

On the other hand, we *are* encouraged to "fear the Lord." That phrase also shows up over 300 times in the Bible. Proverbs 9:10 tells us: "The fear of the Lord is the beginning of wisdom."

Psalm 23:4 ties this together: "Though I walk through the valley of the shadow of death, I will fear no evil, because You (Lord) are with me." I do not fear circumstances; I do not fear men; I only fear the Lord – fear meaning to hold Him in awe and reverence. "Awe-inspiring" is the Hebrew word for fear. According to Jewish scholars, awe is the highest form of worship.

Just as we can choose love over fear, we have other opportunities to choose. God speaks in Deuteronomy 30:19, "Today I am offering you life or death. Choose life, that you and your children may live."

Chuck Swindoll puts our ability to choose this way:

> "The remarkable thing is we have a choice every day regarding the attitude we will embrace for that day. We cannot change our past ...we cannot change the fact that people will act in a certain way. We cannot change the inevitable. The only thing we can do is play on the one string we have, and that is our attitude. I am convinced that life is 10%

what happens to me and 90% how I react to
it. And so it is with you."[28]

As the song so eloquently expresses this freedom
to choose...

> "You can make the mountains ring or make
> the angels cry."

I close this section with the timeless words of Phillips
Brooks' "O Little Town of Bethlehem": "The hopes and
fears of all the years are met in Thee tonight." Jesus's birth,
His arrival on earth, His "first coming" gave the world then
and now a glimpse of God and a living hope. A hope which
can conquer our fears and anxieties. And at the same time,
inspire a healthy fear (awe) of Him, the One who epitomizes
unconditional love.

Now we turn our attention to His second coming.

The Return

I've always been intrigued by the words: "When the
one who left us here returns for us at last." This sentence
fragment was the original reason I included "Get Together"
in this book.

Internet research yields speculation, but not a definitive
interpretation, of these words. Again, we're left to infer the
meaning.

"The one who left us here" seems like a casual way to refer to a Creator. The Bible says the Holy Trinity (God the Father, God the Son, God the Holy Spirit) was present at creation. We tend to think of God the Father as the sole architect of creation. However, Genesis 1:26 says: "Let Us make man in Our image." Who is Us? The Father, Son and Holy Spirit.

The first verse of the Gospel of John reads: "In the beginning was the Word (Jesus), and the Word was with God, and the Word was God." John 1:14 makes sure there is no confusion about the Word: "And the Word became flesh and dwelt among us." The Incarnation; the first coming of Jesus. The second coming - Jesus is "the One who will return for us at last."

Several times in the Gospel accounts of His life, Jesus promises to return for those who believe in Him. In Luke 12:40, He exhorts His disciples: "You too be ready; for the Son of Man is coming at an hour that you do not expect." The majesty of His return is captured in Luke 21:27, "They will see the Son of Man coming in a cloud with power and great glory."

Revelation 22:7 tells us how to prepare for his return. "Behold, I am coming quickly. Blessed is he who heeds the words of the prophecy of this book." Hebrews 9:28 states it plainly: "Christ also, having been offered once to bear the sins of many, shall appear a second time for salvation without reference to sin, to those who eagerly await Him."

So, the real question from the line "The one who left us here returns for us at last" is: Who is "us"? Those who eagerly await Him, who have believed in Him and His words of life, and who have acted on their beliefs, producing good fruit in their allotted years on earth.

Our time is brief, as the song expresses: "We are but a moment's sunlight fading in the grass." Quite similar to James 4:14 – "You are just a vapor that appears for a little while and then vanishes away." Sounds a little depressing, so how do we respond? Either with an attitude of resignation – nothing I do matters – or the opposite. Because we are here for a short time, make every day count, as we are encouraged in Psalm 90:12, "Teach us to number our days, that we may present to Thee a heart of wisdom." Or to put it another way, "Live like you're dying" (Tim McGraw), because you and I are – could be tonight; could be many years down the road. We need to be alert; to be ready for His return. What we do in the meantime *does* matter.

A Final Word

If my interpretation of the beautiful poetry of this song is valid, then the Youngbloods nailed it, consistent with Scripture. We do have choices; we can choose love over fear. We have been put on this earth for a short time. "The One who left us here" will return. He simply asks each one of us to receive Him.

I'm not sure what Jesse Colin Young believes or, for that matter, the original songwriter, Chet Powers. By the way, Powers was granted probation. Still, I suspect when he looked back on the exchange of rights to the song that gained international fame versus a few dollars to pay an attorney, he probably had regrets.

There is an exchange that leads to no regret – giving your life over to "the One who left us here and Who will return for us at last."

CHAPTER 9

"Fire and Rain"

by James Taylor

AS WE COME to the last chapter of the book, I suspect you've been waiting breathlessly for me to reveal my favorite of the nine songs profiled.

Setting aside spiritual implications (ironic since that's the whole focus of the book), which song when it pops up on the radio takes me back and refreshes my mind?

I will withstand the temptation to rank them 1 through 9 and simply reveal the runner-up... "Get Together" and the winner.......... "Fire and Rain." Besides the beautiful melody, the words reinforce the notion that everyone can look back on the hard times that molded us and the good times that we will cherish to the end of our lives.

Background on James Taylor

Taylor was born on March 12, 1948, in Boston. His father was a physician and his mother an aspiring opera singer until she set aside her dreams to raise Taylor and his four siblings.

In 1951, the family moved to Chapel Hill, North Carolina where his father taught at the university. When Taylor was 13, he was sent to Milton Academy, a boarding school in Massachusetts. During his senior year, he became depressed and committed himself to a psychiatric hospital. He later referred to his nine months there as a "lifesaver," although he would still struggle periodically with depression.

Taylor attended Elon College briefly but soon moved to New York. 1966 would prove to be a pivotal year in his life as he formed a band called "The Flying Machine" and he began using heroin.

The Flying Machine quickly broke up; Taylor hit bottom and reached out to his father to rescue him and take him back to North Carolina.

The following year, Taylor moved to London, where he was introduced to Peter Asher, who became his manager and led him to sign with Apple Records. He connected with McCartney and Harrison, who contributed their talents to "Carolina In My Mind."

In 1968, Taylor fell back into his heroin habit, but recovered and moved to California, where he signed with

Warner Brothers Records while retaining Asher as his manager.

The album "Sweet Baby James," which included "Fire and Rain," was released in February 1970.

Taylor has been married three times. His first marriage in 1972 to Carly Simon ended in divorce in 1983. They had two children. Taylor continued to struggle with his drug habit. His second wife, Kathryn Walker, whom he married in 1985, helped him kick his habit, but they divorced in 1996. He married Kim Smedvig in 2001, and they have twin sons Rufus and Henry.

Taylor was inducted into the Rock & Roll Hall of Fame in 2000. He has shared the stage with artists too numerous to recount here. One of the most memorable took place at Madison Square Garden in 2011 where he performed "Fire and Rain" with Taylor Swift, who was named after him.

Background on "Fire and Rain" [29]

During a 2005 interview with NPR, Taylor explained that the song was written in three parts. The first referred to the suicide of a friend, Suzanne Schneer. Taylor didn't learn of the tragedy until six months after the fact, as he was in London at the time and his friends thought it could distract him from his big break (Peter Asher, Apple Records).

The second stanza of the song referred to his struggle to overcome drug addiction and depression, while the final stanza deals with him coming to grips with fame, looking back on the early days, which explains his reference to "flying machines in pieces on the ground."

The song was released as a single in August 1970.

Selected Lyrics [30]

For our purpose, the focus will be on the second stanza:

"Won't you look down upon me, Jesus?
You've got to help me make a stand,
You've just got to see me through another day.
My body's aching and my time is at hand
And I won't make it any other way."

What Does the Bible Say?

These lyrics need no interpretation. They're straightforward. And it should come as no surprise that someone reaching out to Jesus for His help and recognizing He is the only hope is consistent with what the Bible teaches. In fact, one could say it's the heart of the Gospel.

I want to start with the fourth line. The desperation in these words echoes throughout the Bible, most notably in several of the Psalms of David. Even as king, he is often besieged by enemies – external, as well as those in his own household.

Here are just a few examples of David's descriptions of his misery, manifested in his body aches, just as Taylor writes. In similar fashion, there is the realization that only Jesus can deliver from the despair.

Psalm 31:9-10

"I am in distress. My eyes grow weak with sorrow, my soul and body with grief…. my strength has failed."

Psalm 31:14

"<u>But</u> I trust in you, Lord; I say you are my God."

Psalm 69:3

"I am worn out calling for help. My throat is parched. My eyes fail."

Psalm 69:29-30

"<u>But</u> as for me, afflicted and in pain – may your salvation, God, protect me. I will praise God's name in song and glorify Him with thanksgiving."

Psalm 102:5

"In my distress I groan aloud and am reduced to skin and bones."

Psalm 102:12

"<u>But</u> you, Lord, sit enthroned forever; Your renown endures through all generations."

It's not hard to see a pattern here. Depression, despair, anguish. Followed by "But you, Lord" – a change in perspective and a rejuvenated hope in the One who can actually deliver from the depths.

Speaking of which, the Psalms occasionally refer to the depths of despair as the pit. Psalm 88:4 reads: "I am counted among those who go down to the pit; I am like one without strength." The reference to the pit in Psalm 40:2 is more upbeat: "He lifted me up out of the slimy pit, out of the mud and mire; He set my feet on a rock and gave me a firm place to stand."

David was most definitely in the pit. Taylor was often in the pit. I have been in the pit. I bet you have too. Perhaps David's pit was deeper, as he was frequently on the run for his life. In a different way, it seems that Taylor was also on the run for his life, as he grappled with a drug habit and depression for many years. David would emerge from the pit with the simple words "But you, Lord…." The lyrics of "Fire and Rain" echo the same sentiment – "I won't make it any other way." A prevailing theme of this book and, more importantly, God's Book, is crying out to the one true God, the living Lord who hears the cries and answers.

Finally, let's take a look at the chorus:

"Oh, I've seen fire and I've seen rain;
I've seen sunny days that I thought would never end;
I've seen lonely times when I could not find a friend."

I believe this describes all of us. We don't get to choose our circumstances, but we do get to choose whether we focus on the sunny days or the lonely times. I have recently noticed how often a particular word is used in the Bible. That word is "remember." We are exhorted to remember how Jesus has delivered us in the past and will continue to deliver us, from the hard times, from the pit. Internalizing this promise is the key to true contentment. I pray that all those who have read this book are experiencing, or will begin to experience, the contentment and joy that a life with Jesus in your camp and you in His will bring.

I close with a quote from a "Soul Surmise" post:

> "The seventies songwriters without any Christian commitment had an affinity with Jesus. Maybe the 60's rebels had uncovered the real deal." [31]

They had.

FINAL THOUGHTS

I HOPE YOU have enjoyed the journey with these rock & roll icons and perhaps now see their music through a new and different lens.

Observations | The Power of Music

I can't remember what I had for breakfast this morning, but I can certainly recall the lyrics to the songs profiled here, as well as many others from over 50 years ago. Music sticks with you. It stays in your heart. Ephesians 5:19 says: "singing and making melody with your heart to the Lord." Just as I still carry the tunes and words of my favorite rock & roll songs with me, I do the same with my favorite worship songs. What we sing on Sunday stays in my heart throughout the week and gives me a lift.

Music transports us back in time and brings fond memories to our minds. That's what these nine songs do for me. Favorite concerts, TV shows (Ed Sullivan), movies (The Graduate), sharing the music with friends. Music is a language that connects generations and transcends cultures.

Observations | Common Characteristics

When I look back at the lives of these artists, even though I don't know them, I can nevertheless suggest several things they seem to have in common:

- Extremely gifted writers, musicians and performers
- Rebels – a reflection of the times
- Risk-takers / entrepreneurs – would fit almost any aspiring musician
- Political activists – concerned about the poor and oppressed and acted on their behalf
- Messy lives - often impacted by the use of hard drugs
- Most found their way to New York, London or Los Angeles. The world's great cities are a magnet for creative people.
- Finally, and most importantly, in different ways, they seem to have been seekers of spiritual truth, recognizing that this world is not all there is.

Conclusions | Intuition

As I have researched these songs and the musicians who wrote them, I am struck by a sense that there is an explicit or at least an implicit acknowledgement of the unseen world, of the spirit world, among people as diverse as the artists we have profiled. Some accept the centrality of Jesus in this picture; others don't. But based solely on the lyrics, all seemed to have looked inside themselves for a deeper meaning to life, an awareness of a higher power – from the lighthearted "Spirit in the Sky" and "Oh Lord" to the more complex "Sympathy for the Devil" and "My Sweet Lord." Their songs suggest that they were attuned to the spirit within and perhaps would not take issue with Paul's reminder in I Thessalonians 5:23 that we are "spirit, soul and body."

One conclusion therefore is that this intuition, this stirring of the heart, resides in each one of us. The lyrics of the songs in this book reflect that reality. We should ask: Who put the stirring there? I submit it is the God of the Bible.

We often hear that Christianity is a leap of faith. That's true, but perhaps rather than one big leap, for some it could be a series of smaller leaps.

The leaps could look something like this:

Intuition (stirring) →
   → Creator God →
     → who intervenes →
       → God who reveals Himself in Jesus

The first leap is an intuitive awareness of the unseen something or someone. It *is* hard to believe in the unseen world; it is just as hard to discount its existence altogether. I believe we were all created with the awareness of the unseen – this connection to spirit. Blaise Pascal, 17th century mathematician and philosopher, put it this way: "Inside the heart of each man is a God-shaped vacuum."

The stirring in your heart can produce turmoil or calm, a serenity if you surrender your heart and soul to Jesus. St. Augustine expressed the calm that comes from a relationship with Jesus this way: "You have made us for yourself, O Lord, and our hearts are restless until they rest in You."

Conclusions | More Than a Book – The Original Blueprint

I quote from the Bible more than 80 times in this book. A conclusion you may have rightly drawn is that I try to live my life and inform my world view through a biblical lens. Why? Because I believe it's the Word of the Creator for His creation; the Instruction Manual for our lives provided by the One who gave us life. It seems wise to familiarize ourselves with it. I hope reading this book has instilled a desire in you to take your first dive or perhaps rekindled a desire to take a deeper dive into the question: "What does the Bible say?" This is why I closed each one of the chapters in this manner. This is the perspective that matters.

The Bible is not just a good book full of helpful advice just as Jesus was not just a man who exhibited wisdom and compassion.

Absolute proof of these notions is not possible, but consider the following:

I wrote an article entitled "Headscratchers." The gist of it is that the Bible is filled with such odd stories and details that if men were trying to invent a book to honor their God, they certainly would not have included many of the difficult, and yes bizarre, passages that are found in the Bible. My conclusion was that the Bible must be the inspired Word of God.

One can find a more scholarly approach in Josh McDowell's book "Evidence That Demands a Verdict."[32] His starting point for the rest of the book is the uniqueness of the Bible because if it can be viewed as authentic, then the deity of Jesus and the reality of His life, death and resurrection naturally flows from this conclusion. The book made a compelling case for the uniqueness of the Bible and hence its claim to be the Word of God. Let me highlight just a few key points:

- Written over a 1600-year span
- By 40 authors from different walks of life – fishermen, physicians, kings, shepherds, prophets
- On three continents
- In three languages

And yet it holds together with clear, consistent themes from Genesis to Revelation. The central theme is God's pursuit of relationship with His creation, ultimately through

His Son. The Bible points to God's Son, Jesus, as the way to eternal life and to a life of contentment irrespective of circumstances while we reside on this earth.

Conclusions | Jesus Is THE Rock

The last three songs profiled in this book reflect an appreciation of Jesus as the One to turn to in times of trouble – the One who is your friend, who forgives, who comforts, and who will return.

In his seminal book "Mere Christianity," C.S. Lewis puts it this way: "I am trying here to prevent anyone saying the really foolish thing that people often say about Him (that is, Christ): 'I'm ready to accept Jesus as a great moral teacher, but I don't accept His claim to be God.' That is the one thing we must not say. A man who was merely a man and said the sort of things Jesus said would not be a great moral teacher. He would either be a lunatic or else He would be the Devil of Hell. You must make your choice. Either this man was, and is, the Son of God or else a madman or something worse. You can shut Him up for a fool, you can spit at Him and kill Him as a demon, or you can fall at His feet and call Him Lord and God. But let us not come up with any patronizing nonsense about His being a great human teacher. He has not left that option open to us." [33]

Conclusions | Jesus was who He said He was – the Son of God.

In one short sentence, Colossians 1:15 ties together Lewis's claim about Jesus and a theme that permeates this book - wrestling with the unseen world: "Jesus is the image of the invisible God."

Where Do You Stand?

I wrote this book because these ideas have stirred in my heart for years. I enjoy the rock & roll classics from the 60s and 70s. Even more, I enjoy my Christian faith. As I contemplated the lyrics of these songs, I became more and more intrigued as to how my Christian world view might intersect with some of the lyrics. I decided to share my conclusions with anyone who chose to read my book.

I opened the book with a few fun questions about your favorites from this era. But to wrap up, let me pose more consequential questions.

- Is there a stirring in your heart?
- If so, who put it there?
- Could the Bible actually be the Word of God? Is it plausible? Is it probable?
- In Matthew 16, we find Jesus and His disciples talking about who the people say that He is. But

then He put the question directly to them - "Who do *you* say that I am?" How do *you* answer that question?

I am humbled that you took the time to read and engage with my book. Thank you.

EPILOGUE

NO SEQUEL IS planned for this book. And I won't sue you for copyright infringement if you choose to take the concept and run with it.

Other songs I considered: "American Pie" with Don McLean's lyrics "and the three men I admire most – the Father, Son and Holy Ghost...", Led Zeppelin's "Stairway to Heaven", Neil Diamond's "Brother Love's Traveling Salvation Show," Doobie Brothers' "Jesus Is Just Alright With Me," and John Denver's "Rocky Mountain High" ("talk to God and listen to the casual reply").

Country music certainly offers a bunch of songs to be considered. Many country artists sing gospel music, which I would exclude for this purpose, but let me offer a couple of examples to get the discussion going with respect to this genre.

Who knew that Jimmy Buffet and Job shared a similar view of life. I love the closing line of "He Went to Paris," where Buffet sings "Some of it's magic; some of it's tragic, but I've had a good life all the way." About 3,000 years earlier,

Job captured a similar sentiment, when he acknowledged, "The Lord gives, the Lord takes away; blessed be the name of the Lord."

David Allan Coe's "You Never Even Call Me By My Name" closes with a sentence familiar to many country music fans that makes no sense if you're not a fan. "I was drunk the day my mom got out of prison, so I went to pick her up in the rain, but before I could get to the station in my pickup truck, she got runned over by a damned old train." But the words I'm referring to from the same song are "The only time I know I'll hear David Allan Coe is when Jesus has his final judgment day." Yep.

Have fun with this. Add your own. Write a book.

APPENDIX I

My Answers to the Questions in the Introduction

SINCE IT'S MY book, I can bend the rules and offer two or more answers to each question.

Best Concerts I attended

- Bruce Springsteen at Cameron Indoor Stadium (Durham, North Carolina) just after the album "Born to Run" was released.
- Paul McCartney at United Spirit Arena (Lubbock, Texas) in 2015. Started his U.S. tour there to pay tribute to Lubbock's own Buddy Holly and his influence on the Beatles.

The Songs That Most Defined This Era

- Hey Jude
- Sweet Caroline
- Born to Be Wild

The Best Rock & Roll Songs

- The three above that defined the era plus
- Free Bird
- Stairway to Heaven
- Hotel California
- Satisfaction

The Best Rock & Roll Albums

- Dark Side of the Moon
- Abbey Road
- Born to Run
- Who's Next

APPENDIX II

Take Time to Reflect

Chapter 1 – "Spirit in the Sky"

1. Is this world all there is, or is there an afterlife?
2. Which is easier to believe? Why?
3. Which do you believe?
4. If you believe there is "a place that's best," are you ready?

Chapter 2 – "Sympathy for the Devil"

1. Do you sense a battle for your soul?
2. How would you describe it?
3. Who is winning?

Chapter 3 – "Oh Lord, Won't You Buy Me a Mercedes Benz?"

1. Have you ever prayed for material things? Was the prayer answered? How?
2. Do you distinguish between wants and needs?
3. We are all materialists to varying degrees. Assess your level of materialism.
4. How do you define the abundant life? How do you define success?
5. Are your definitions consistent with what the Bible teaches?

Chapter 4 – "Imagine"

1. Stretch your imagination. Describe your "room," your "daily routine," and your interactions with fellow citizens of Heaven.
2. If God created this majestic, intricate world that man has made a mess of, try to imagine the jubilation, the euphoria of Heaven. What will it look like when everything is set right, when we witness perfect justice and experience perfect mercy?
3. Is an earthly utopia possible? Why or why not?

Chapter 5 – "Money"

1. Identify idols in your life.

2. Is money one of your idols? How about financial security?

3. How would you have responded to Jesus's challenge to the rich young ruler to sell everything, give to the poor and follow Him?

4. The Bible says: "You are not your own; you were bought with a price." Does that comfort you or trouble you? Why?

Chapter 6 – "My Sweet Lord"

1. Conduct your own 10-minute internet research…. What do the world's major religions believe about Jesus?

2. Recall Harrison's quote that "all religions are branches of the same tree." What makes Christianity unique?

3. Would you characterize Christianity as exclusive? Why or why not?

Chapter 7 – "Mrs. Robinson"

1. Do you need to forgive anyone?

2. Do you need forgiveness?

3. Think about forgiving others in the context of the words of Job 18:4 – "you who tear yourself to pieces in anger"

Chapter 8 – "Get Together"

1. Do you believe in a literal Second Coming of Christ?
2. Do you think it will happen in your lifetime?
3. Describe what you think you will see.
4. What is your biggest fear? How can it be conquered?

Chapter 9 – "Fire and Rain"

1. Are there times in your life when you have truly been in the pit? What was it like? How did you get in the pit? How did you get out?
2. Is there a distinction between simple words of prayer to Jesus and crying out to Jesus? If so, does it matter and how would you describe the distinction?

Select Verses to Consider from THE Book*

Matthew 11:28

"Come to Me, all who are weary and heavy-laden, and I will give you rest."

John 10:10

"I have come that you might have life and have it abundantly."

John 15:11

"These things I have spoken to you so that My joy may be in you, and that your joy may be full."

Hebrews 1:1-2

"God, after He spoke long ago to the fathers in the prophets in many portions and in many ways, in these last days has spoken to us in His Son."

Ecclesiastes 3:11

"He has set eternity in the heart of man."

Psalm 46:10

"Be still and know that I am God."

Psalm 23:4

"Even though I walk through the valley of the shadow of death, I will fear no evil, for You are with me."

Proverbs 4:23

"Guard your heart with all diligence, for out of it spring the issues of life."

Jeremiah 29:11

"For I know the plans that I have for you, to give you a future and a hope."

*Consider these scripture verses if you are evaluating the trustworthiness of the Bible. Internalize these verses if you already believe. Internalize, for me, means I can readily call them to mind when I need the encouragement and the reminders of how God has delivered me time and again.

NOTES

Chapter 1

1   Greenbaum, Norman, 'Spirit in the Sky,' Spirit in the Sky, Reprise Records, 1969

2   Lyrics.com, STANDS4 LLC, 2024. "Spirit in the Sky Lyrics," accessed November 27, 2024. https://www.lyrics.com/lyric-lf/436597/Norman+Greenbaum/Spirit+in+the+Sky

Chapter 2

3   Mick Jagger and The Rolling Stones, "Sympathy for the Devil," Beggars Banquet, Decca Records, 1968

4   Writer/s: Keith Richards, Mick Jagger, Publisher: Abkco Music Inc., BMG Rights Management, Lyrics licensed and provided by LyricFind, November 27, 2024

5   Lewis, C.S., The Screwtape Letters, New York, Harper Collins, 1942

Chapter 3

6   Joplin, Janis, "Mercedes Benz," Pearl, Columbia, 1971

7   Lyrics.com, STANDS4 LLC, 2024. "Mercedes Benz Lyrics," accessed November 27, 2024. https://www.lyrics.com/lyric/19553627/Janis+Joplin/Mercedes+Benz

8   Wilkinson, Bruce. The Prayer of Jabez: Breaking Through to the Blessed Life, Colorado Springs, Multnomah Books, 2000, p. 24. *Emphasis added*

Chapter 4

9   https://www.latimes.com/opinion/op-ed/la-oe-beatles-quotes-20140209-story.html, accessed 11/27/2024

10   https://www.brainyquote.com/quotes/paul_mccartney_349149, accessed 11/27/2024

11   https://www.facebook.com/johnlennon/posts/the-quarrymenthe-quarry-men-is-the-name-of-the-group-before-it-turned-into-the-b/837690914380031/, accessed 11/272024

12   Lennon, John, "Imagine," Imagine, Apple Records, 1971

13   Mercy Me, "I Can Only Imagine," Track 13 on I Can Only Imagine: The Very Best of MercyMe, INO Records, 1999

14   https://genius.com/Mercyme-i-can-only-imagine-lyrics, accessed 11/27/2024

Chapter 5

15   https://parade.com/tv/archie-bunker-quotes#:~:text=%22All%20of%20them%20old%20Bible, It's%20true

16   https://ultimateclassicrock.com/pink-floyd-money/

Chapter 6

17   Glazer, Mitchell (1977). "Growing Up at 33⅓: The George Harrison Interview." Crawdaddy (February)

18   https://www.backtogodhead.in/my-sweet-lord/,   accessed 12/30/2024

19   Harrison, George, "My Sweet Lord," All Things Must Pass, Apple Records, 1970

20   https://www.goodreads.com/quotes/599126-all-religions-are-br anches-of-one-big-tree-it-doesn-t, accessed 11/27/2024

21   Packer, J.I., Knowing God, Fiftieth Anniversary Edition, Downers Grove, InterVarsity Press, 2023

Chapter 7

22   Nichols, Mike. 1967. The Graduate. United States. Embassy Pictures

23   https://jewishmom.com/2021/12/16/his-mothers-words-tha t-singer-paul-simon-never-forgot/, assessed 11/27/2024

24   Simon, Paul and Garfunkel, Arthur, "Mrs. Robinson," Bookends, Columbia Records, 1968

Chapter 8

25   The Youngbloods, "Get Together," The Youngbloods, RCA Victor, 1967

26   https://songmeanings.com/songs/view/3530822107858539677/ Accessed 11/27/2024

27   https://www.goldminemag.com/interviews/jesse-colin-young-still-a-youngblood, accessed 12/30/2024

28   https://www.goodreads.com/quotes/267482-the-longer-i-liv e-the-more-i-realize-the-impact, accessed 11/27/2024

Chapter 9

[29] Taylor, James, "Fire and Rain," Sweet Baby James, Warner Bros Records, 1970

[30] https://genius.com/James-taylor-fire-and-rain-lyrics, accessed 11/27/2024

[31] https://stocki.typepad.com/soulsurmise/2017/09/that-time-when-james-taylor-cried-out-to-jesus.html, accessed 11/27/24

Final Thoughts

[32] McDowell, Josh & McDowell, Sean, "Evidence That Demands a Verdict, Life-Changing Truth for a Skeptical World," Nashville, Thomas Nelson Publishers, 2017

[33] Lewis, C.S., "Mere Christianity," New York, Harper One Publishers, 1980, p. 52

ABOUT THE AUTHOR

FRANK GARROTT is an accomplished businessman as well as a man of passion and purpose. Throughout his career, he has worked in financial services and consulting, as well as missions and ministry. His heart is to honor Christ by caring for the orphans and vulnerable child populations, and by stimulating others through thought-provoking conversation. His goal: to draw people to discover the One who changed his life.

Frank claims no qualifications to write this book. He's not an author – this is his first book. He's not seminary trained, although he did recall a night course that he took on homiletics but now can't remember what that word means. He's not a religious scholar, although he did take and pass two religion courses in college. Despite three years of high school Spanish, he makes no claim to be a linguist. Doesn't know a word of Hebrew or Greek. For that matter, doesn't know much Spanish. On the other hand, he has read and pondered the Bible a lot and come under the tutelage of wonderful mentors.

Since 2018, Frank has been working for a non-profit called Both Ends Believing, whose focus is providing a technology platform to the child welfare ministries of developing nations to enable them to manage their orphan and vulnerable child population with the objective of seeing these children in safe and loving families.

Prior to Both Ends Believing, Frank served as the President of the Gladney Center for Adoption for ten years. Before that, he had a 30-year career in financial services and consulting. He served on the Gladney and BEB boards, as well as five other non-profit boards, one centered on work at the United Nations and the others focused on child welfare.

He received his B.A. from Duke University and his MBA from the University of Texas at Austin.

Frank lives in Dallas, Texas with his wife Lynne. They have five adult children, all of whom are married to wonderful spouses, and two grandchildren.

www.ingramcontent.com/pod-product-compliance
Lightning Source LLC
Chambersburg PA
CBHW060239030426
42335CB00014B/1530